THE EXTIRPATION
OF IDOLATRY
IN PERU

THE EXTIRPATION
OF IDOLATRY
IN PERU

by Father Pablo Joseph de Arriaga

Translated and Edited by
L. CLARK KEATING

UNIVERSITY OF KENTUCKY PRESS

The publication of this book has been made possible partly
through a grant from the Margaret Voorhies Haggin Trust,
established in memory of her husband, James Ben Ali Haggin.

PREFACE

THE PROBLEMS of translation—the transfer to a second language of the message, mood, and flavor of the first—have an inevitable fascination for most students of foreign languages. It was with some eagerness, therefore, that I undertook to translate Father Arriaga's book on the religion of the Incas. It soon became obvious as the work progressed that a fund of knowledge other than linguistic would be required, and so I had to draw constantly on what knowledge of Peru I had acquired when I lived there from 1960 to 1962. Much other miscellaneous information was also needed, and for this I relied on colleagues and friends.

Father Joseph cannot be called a difficult writer. In his book there are few obscure passages. He usually said what he meant and said it simply. He should be easy to read, but he is not always so easy as he looks. Despite the fact that he was a teacher of rhetoric he has, by modern standards, some conspicuous defects of style. One of these is a habit of stringing together many disparate ideas in a single sentence. He overworked his few conjunctions not only in the middle of a sentence but at the beginning. The Spanish equivalents of *but, and,* and *for* are ever present. To retain them all would result in bad English. To eliminate them all would be not to translate but to rewrite Father Arriaga, a temptation a translator must stoutly resist. There is also the matter of active and passive voice. Spanish uses the active more frequently than English does, and when it wants an impersonal passive it relies on its handy reflexive. Here again the translator must strike a happy medium. With the exception of this sort of change, the usual ground rules have been observed: no rewriting merely to "improve" the style. The translator who does otherwise deserves to have applied to him the well-known Italian maxim, *traduttore, traditore,* which means that to translate is to betray. For these reasons I have left Father

Arriaga pretty much as I found him: an unskilled writer whose sincerity and piety were his chief assets.[a]

The text followed here is that of the edition published in Lima in 1920, edited by Horacio H. Urteaga. I have compared this edition with that of 1621, and except in those places where Urteaga corrected an obvious error on Father Arriaga's part I have followed the spelling of the earlier edition when the two have not agreed. The footnotes of the 1920 edition have been translated but are essentially unchanged, although the citations of published materials have been modernized somewhat. These footnotes are designated by numbers. Footnotes added by the translator are designated by letters and follow after the notes of the Spanish edition. Comments and emendations by the translator have been placed in brackets.

Father Arriaga himself compiled a short list of Quechua words that he had not defined in the text. His glossary has been expanded in this translation to include all Quechua words and their definitions. There has been no such full listing of the Quechua terms and their meanings in any edition of Arriaga's book; in the 1920 edition, information concerning the etymology of words as well as their meanings was provided by the editor, but only in a sporadic fashion in the notes. All such information, whether provided in the original text or added by editors, is scattered and usually offered only once, despite the fact that many of these words were used more than once, in widely separated parts of the book. The reader will find, therefore, that a central glossary that pulls this information together in one place far surpasses a system of cross-references between notes—an approach attempted but not by any means comprehensively done by the Spanish editor. This glossary, which is on pp. 175-85, should save the reader no small amount of effort.

The Quechua words are italicized only on their first use in the text; thereafter, they appear in roman type. In the foot-

---

[a] Readers interested in the problems, practical as well as theoretical, which beset the translator may read the excellent book, *On Translation*, edited by Reuben Brower (Cambridge: Harvard University Press, 1959).

notes, both those of the Spanish edition of 1920 and of the translator, words are italicized whenever they are themselves the subject of discussion; translations, either from Spanish or Quechua to English or the reverse, are enclosed in double quotes.

The word *huaca*, which assumes in this text the status of a loan word in both English and Spanish, is therefore never italicized. It appears frequently in the text and it refers to a sacred object or idol. It is first explained in the Spanish text on p. 15, n. 2, which in this text is p. 20, n. 17. A fuller definition of the word is found in the glossary.

The translator's gratitude is hereby expressed to the Association of American University Presses, whose generous grant has made possible the translation of this book.

Lexington, Kentucky   L. CLARK KEATING
October 1967

CONTENTS

INTRODUCTION

SPAIN AND PERU. In picturing the country with which our author is concerned, we must remember that geographically Peru was for him a vaguely defined territory which included at least as much as all of present-day Ecuador, all of Bolivia, and the northern half of Chile, as well as what is now called Peru. From the early Spanish point of view, which does not differ greatly from that of the non-Indian tourist of today, greater Peru was a grim, inhospitable land of impassable mountains and chasms and airless, treeless plateaus. Only by settling on the coast have newcomers found the land habitable. Only by trusting themselves to narrow rock ledges called roads, or by pitting man and airplane against winds and peaks second only to those of the Himalayas, does man from other continents venture today into the fastnesses where the Incas chose to live. This was the country in which the tough, tireless, and zealous monks of the sixteenth and seventeenth centuries walked and rode horseback, visiting and revisiting remote Indian villages, founding churches and missions, preaching, catechizing, and confessing. No easy generalization about these men of religion should be attempted. We know from history, and we can infer from the preachments of our author against unworthy priests, that many of them were just that: unworthy priests, more anxious for their fortune than for the good of the Indians, hankering more after the fleshpots than after righteousness. The truly dedicated, among whom we must count Father Pablo Joseph de Arriaga, worked for the saving of souls as devoutly as they knew how. They worked among the members of a race whose customs and language were alien to them, and they worked at great personal risk in a difficult country.

The Church in Peru. From the sixteenth to the nineteenth century the Black Legend, or the systematic denigration and calumny of Spain by Anglo-Saxon historians, obscured almost entirely the civilizing work of the Spanish church during and after the conquest of the New World. With the present century, Spanish and purportedly neutral historians have gone so far in the opposite direction that there are scholars who would have us believe that the Indian was better off as a quasi-slave under the system of tutelage known as *encomiendas* than he was as a quasi-free man in the socialized regime of the Incas. The truth is somewhere in the middle, as usual. We cannot blink at the rapacity of mineowners and landowners and the greed and lechery of some of the priests and simply assure ourselves that all was well in Peru under Spanish rule. Still, the virtuous character and good deeds of some of the honorable exceptions to the general rapacity are remarkable. If, as William James has said, a religion deserves to be judged by its best rather than its worst, then men like Father Arriaga prove that the Spanish church deserves a respect untinged with condescension. It was no small achievement for our author to speak of qualified Jesuits of Indian blood, working with him in the first two decades of the seventeenth century. Such a fact contrasts in Spain's favor, to put it mildly, with the founding of Dartmouth College as late as 1769 as a school for Indians in the North American colonies, or the founding of the Carlisle Indian School in 1879. It is true that the circumstances in the two continents were different; still, there is no evading the fact that in the northern continent the Indian was hustled out of the way. In South America he became, for better or worse, involved in European culture.

The Spanish means of controlling the Indian population of their new territory was almost as efficient as the rule of the Inca, and far more ruthless. Most of the fertile land, or the land containing minerals, was vested in landlords to whom the adjacent Indian population was "entrusted" for schooling in Spanish ways. These holdings were known as *encomiendas*. Where the land was thought to be useless, districts were set up, each of which was presided over by a *corregidor*, or magistrate, who had life-and-death power over the Indians in his district. Indians who did not fall into either of these categories were "free," but every village had its *fiscal,* or crown agent, to collect taxes and report to the viceroy all the important occurrences in his area. The clerical arm was no less well organized. By 1586 the country had been divided into four dioceses, and beneath these were parishes to which many Indian towns were attached for purposes of administration. The plan was to have a church and a priest in every important town in the viceroyalty. New areas were named *doctrinas,* or missions, until a more regular organization could take over. Meanwhile, paganism flourished, not only in remote areas but also, as our author makes clear, right in full view of the ministers of the Christian religion. It was with this knowledge that Father Arriaga supported so strongly the establishment of what he called "visits," but which, as we can see from the context, were more on the order of a religious inspection, with all the functions and powers of an ecclesiastical court. It is a description of these visits and of the information obtained thereby about Indian idolatry that is the burden of Father Arriaga's book.

Father Arriaga's Attitude toward the Indians. Quite obviously, Father Arriaga regarded the Indian culture as inferior to that of Spain. This is apparent in what he says and in what he does not say. But he was not particularly culture conscious. When he thought about culture at all it was in connection with his problems as a missionary and teacher. He was aware of the strength of patterns of behavior "absorbed with one's mother's milk," as he puts it. Such patterns, he tells us, are hard to eradicate. He fears that even well-educated Indians cannot be trusted with certain chores, such as idol-smashing. But nowhere in his book does he indulge in any racist nonsense or imply that the Indian, *qua* Indian, is a lesser man than those who are trying to convert him. Nor is he fanatical. He does not want the fragments of a broken idol to be burned because of any sentiment of hatred but because he has learned through practical experience that if this is not done the job will soon have to be done all over again. The sorcerers and ministers of idolatry present a problem, of course, for if they backslide into the pagan cult they generally take the people with them. For this reason he sees no recourse but to shave their heads, to whip them, to exile them, or to imprison them, but he is careful to add that most of them are simply old people who have no other way to make a living and that we should therefore not be too hard on them. This is refreshingly human. He is equally human as well as shrewd when he warns his fellow priests that the expensive ornaments and beautiful garments which are taken away from the Indians to discourage the pagan cult must never remain in the hands of those who confiscate them. "If we do this how will the Indians believe in our sincerity?" he asks. He is eager at all times that the Indians should realize that everything that is done to them, including punishments, is for their own good. The Indian, in other words, was neither an object of scorn or an object of pity for Father Arriaga. The Indian was a soul to be won in the unshaken belief that Christianity, as the Roman Catholic Church taught it, was the one true religion. No cultural relativism tempered this view, but Father Arriaga expresses frequent sympathy for the plight of the Indians and for Indian achievements, and a fundamental respect for the Indians as men. He was convinced that if the Indians but knew the truth they would cling to it.

Father Arriaga's Book. Father Arriaga wrote his work on Indian idolatry in the years immediately following 1616 and 1617, for he refers to events of those years in which he has taken part. His book was published in Lima in 1621 with the permission of all the requisite authorities. It was reprinted in Buenos Aires in 1910 and was next printed in Lima in 1920, edited by Dr. Horacio H. Urteaga. In commenting on the book, Urteaga makes no mention of the fact that the second edition corrected a serious error of the first. The printer of the original edition dropped four numbers from his pagination, viz., 52, 53, 54, 55. This makes his edition appear four pages shorter than its successor, though the text is the same.

The edition of 1920 uses a modern typeface and eliminates

two short pious exercises entitled "Modus et forma recon-
ciliando excomunicatos" (four pages), and a "Litaniae vitae
et passionis domini nostri Iesu Christ" (four pages), which are
appended to Father Arriaga's text. The principles and practices employed by the editor are a little obscure. His policy
with regard to modernizing the text is quite inconsistent.
Words such as *más, también,* and *después,* and present parti-
ciples to which object pronouns are attached (e.g., *hallándola*)
generally but not always have the graphic accent added in
accordance with modern usage. The use of the tilde to
replace a final *n* is abolished, for the most part, but this is
sometimes done without taking into account its implication
and then *llamā* is rendered *llama* instead of *llaman.* *Debajo*
is written instead of *debaxo,* the older form, but *casalla* and
similar expressions are not changed to the modern *casarla,*
nor is *dizen* changed to *dicen.* For reasons that are not
apparent, the *que* of the earlier editions is rendered as *q',*
as if there were a deliberate attempt to make the text archaic
even when it is not. Verbs are equally inconsistent. At times
the auxiliary *à* is changed to *ha,* at other times it is written as *a;*
avria has had an accent added to make it *avría,* but it has not
been given the modern form *habría.* Double *ss* is sometimes
simplified as *s* and sometimes not, e.g., in a single paragraph,
p. 57 (1920 edition), we find *frase* and *frasse.* The earlier text
used *frasse* in both instances. Misspellings occur in the 1920
edition which were not in the earlier ones, e.g., p. 50, *Indos*
for *Indios.* The chaotic capitalization of the earlier editions
has been for the most part retained and the use of the comma
is not at all improved in the latest edition. Obvious misprints
have not been corrected, e.g., p. 57 (1920 edition), gives
desollandola, as do the other two editions. Obviously this
should read *desgollándola.* It is true that such small errors are
of minor importance, but they could have been corrected with
ease.

Father Arriaga's book has long been on the list of books
that would be useful in English translation. It is cited by
Philip Ainsworth Means as an important book for the study

of the early history of Peru, and Dr. Curtis Wilgus notes its importance in his bibliography of source materials for the study of Peru. It is to be hoped that the present translation will be found useful not only by scholars but also by those many persons who, for one reason or another, find themselves ever more fascinated by the story of the Incas.

Bibliography. The discoveries and publications in the field of Peruvian archeology and anthropology have been multiplying so rapidly of late that to append to this translation a list of even the most important titles would go far beyond the translator's intent or competence. Listed below are the works that have been found useful and illuminating in one way or another in the preparation of this volume.

Baudin, Louis. *A Socialist Empire: The Incas of Peru,* trans. Katherine Woods (New York: Van Nostrand, 1961).

Bushnell, G. H. S. *Peru* (New York: Praeger, 1963).

Cieza de León, Pedro. *Del Señorío de los Incas* (Buenos Aires: Solar, 1943).

De la Vega, Garcilaso. *Los comentarios reales de los Incas* (Lima: Gil, 1941-1946).

Gibson, Charles. *The Inca Concept of Sovereignty and the Spanish Administration in Peru* (Austin: University of Texas Press, 1948).

Mason, J. Alden. *The Ancient Civilizations of Peru* (New York: Penguin Books, 1957).

Means, Philip Ainsworth. *Fall of the Inca Empire* (New York: Gordian Press, 1964).

Prescott, W. H. *The Conquest of Peru* (New York: Random House, n.d.).

Stevenson, Robert. *The Music of Peru* (Washington: The Pan-American Union, 1959).

Zimmerman, Arthur F. *Francisco de Toledo, Fifth Viceroy of Peru* (Caldwell, Idaho: Caxton Press, 1938).

Father Pablo Joseph de Arriaga[a]

FATHER Pablo Joseph de Arriaga, of the Society of Jesus, a
Biscayan of noble antecedents, was a native of the city of
Vergara, where, according to his early biographers, he was
born in 1564. But the Fathers Backer maintain that he entered
the novitiate of his order in his native city of Ocaña in 1679.
(It was in 1579 that Father Arriaga entered the novitiate. He
was only fifteen years old at the time.) He continued his
studies in the Colegio de Madrid, where he was given his
orders, and he then served in the *colegios* of Ocaña and
Vergara. By permission of the Council of the Indies he
embarked for Peru on September 6, 1584. After a pleasant
voyage he reached Lima in June 1585 in the company of five
other fathers and fourteen brothers sent by General Claudio
Aquaviva. These twenty religious came under the supervision
of Father Andrés López, who had been sent as a procurator
to Rome and who died in Panama on his return. Before he
died he entrusted the supervision of the religious and the
care of the documents he was carrying from Rome to Father
Samaniego, who was one of those traveling to Peru. We take
these facts from the *Libro de ingresos de religiosos de la
Compañía de Jesús*, a most valuable original document preserved in the Manuscript Division of the National Library. In
this document it is stated that Father Arriaga came from the
Jesuit province of Toledo.

On his arrival in Lima, his Provincial, Father Atienza,
assigned him to teach rhetoric in the schools of the Society.
In 1588 he was named rector of the Colegio de San Martín,
founded in 1582. He kept this post for twenty-four years,
alternating it with that of rector of the Colegio de Arequipa, a
post which he held from 1612 to 1615. At about that time the
Provincial Father, Juan Sebastián, decided to send members of
the Society to carry on missions in the Indian villages of the
archbishopric. They were to be accompanied by visitors of

idolatry,[b] and Father Arriaga was assigned to one of these missions.

He proved to be a zealous missionary and performed his task in an admirable manner, not limiting himself to catechizing and preaching to the Indians but also carrying out profound investigations concerning the religion of the natives and bequeathing us in print the fruit of his investigations. Both the missionaries and the visitors realized, however, that everything that could be done for the conversion of the natives would be in vain if the evil were not extirpated by the roots, and that the only remedy was the Christian education of Indian children and the severe punishment of adult idolaters. After discussing the matter with the Viceroy—the Prince of Esquilache—Archbishop Lobo Guerrero and the Provincial of the Society agreed that two schools should be established for the sons of the chieftains, one in Lima, to be called El Príncipe, not so much in honor of the Prince of Esquilache as in honor of Prince Philip, heir to the throne of Spain, and another in Cuzco, called San Bernardo. There was also to be a house of detention, called Santa Cruz, within the capital district. The plans for this house, as well as its actual construction, were entrusted by the Viceroy to Father Arriaga, as he himself avers. Both the schools and the house were ready and functioning in 1619, under the management of the Jesuits.

In 1601 Father Arriaga returned to Europe with Father Diego de Torres Bollo to serve as procurator for the Society. He came back in 1603 with twenty-four religious whom Father Torres Bollo had gotten together to bring to Peru with the permission of the Council of the Indies, dated December 1602.

Father Arriaga not only divided his time between teaching young people, pious activities, and catechizing the Indians but

[a] This brief biographical sketch, included in the 1920 edition of *Extirpación de la idolatría en el Perú,* first appeared as an article in the *Revista histórica de Lima,* 1919.

[b] The word *visitor* ("visitador") is used for these officials, whose duty it was to ferret out, report, and destroy manifestations of idolatry. Perhaps the word *inspector* would be more in harmony with the function performed, but I have retained the word *visitor* throughout. See also *infra,* p. 17, n. *d.*

also wrote and published several important works which deserve the honor of being reprinted. One of these, which has given a universal reputation to its author, was his *Extirpación de la idolatría en el Perú,* an inexhaustible fount of information for the historian concerning the religion and the customs of the Indians of this country. This was the result of his investigations among the Indians during the so-called visits of idolatry, carried out in the Archbishopric of Lima by him as a zealous churchman, in the company of Father Luís de Teruel and Dr. Avendaño and with the encouragement of the Archbishop, Don Bartolomé Lobo Guerrero. In the *Revista histórica* (Vol. VI, No. 2) we have published a most interesting paper, hitherto unpublished, which was found among the manuscripts of the National Library, entitled *Misión de los Indios huachos y yauyos,* which is evidently from the pen of Father Teruel. This we infer from the fact that the aforementioned cleric was then going about on missions in that province, and that excerpts from a letter written to Father Arriaga, and inserted by the latter in his book, coincide exactly with the information concerning the dealings of the Indians with the Devil, given by the author of the manuscript to which we refer.

The *Extirpación de la idolatría en el Perú* was printed in Lima in 1621 in the print shop of Jerónimo de Contreras and is extraordinarily rare. Only a few copies of the book are known to exist in foreign libraries, as for example, London, Paris, Santiago de Chile, etc. In Lima the only known copy is in the Library of San Marcos University, thereby enriching it along with the other bibliographic jewels which formed the personal library of Don Leonardo Villar and which were acquired by that institution. In 1910 the Argentine professor, Don Pedro N. Arata, had a facsimile printing made in Buenos Aires, using for the purpose a photostatic copy made from the copy in the Bibliothèque nationale in Paris, but his edition was limited to 120 numbered copies, distributed among his friends. One of these copies was dedicated to Don Ricardo Palma, who very generously donated it to the National Library, which did not own a copy of the Lima edition.

The Archbishop of Lima, Don Pedro de Villagómez, made much use of Father Arriaga's work in his *Carta pastoral sobre las idolatrías de los Indios,* as he frankly declares. The illustrious Jesuit, Father Calancha, has also used the work profitably, as have many others.

During his stay in Rome, during the years 1601 and 1602, Father Arriaga printed in the eternal city a spiritual guide with the title *Manual de oraciones y avisos,* a book which was much in demand. A few years later, in 1608, this was reprinted in Lima by Francisco del Canto, the second printer of the Peruvian metropolis. The work consists of 3 pages of front matter and 28 unnumbered pages, 2 pages of illustrations and 400 pages of text. Both editions are very rare. Other editions were printed in Seville of the *Directorio espiritual,* one in 1617, published by Francisco Lira, and another in 1631. In the first of these, included among the unnumbered pages are 12 pages containing a *Sumario de las Reglas de las Congregaciones fundadas en el Colegio de San Martín.* Loose copies of this summary exist, perhaps printed separately.

Father Arriaga translated from Italian to Spanish the *Tratado de la perfección religiosa y de la obligación que todos los religiosos tienen de aspirar a ella,* by the Jesuit Father Lucas Pinelo. This translation was printed in Valladolid in 1604, reprinted in Barcelona in 1610, in Madrid in 1611, and in Seville in 1751.

Finally, in Leon in 1619, Father Arriaga gave to the celebrated printing house of the illustrious Horacio Cardón his *Rhetoris Christiana,* dedicated to the Royal Colegio de San Martín, in Lima. This book consists of 11 pages of front matter, followed by 391 pages of text. Of this there is one copy in the National Library.

The following works by Father Arriaga have remained unpublished:

"Libro de ejercicios espirituales y devociones con instrucciones para aquellos que se educan en nuestros seminarios," a manuscript of 260 pages, cited by the Fathers Backer, which existed in autograph in the old Library of Lima.

"De Beatae Virgine y de Angele Custode," which was also in the library of Lima before its destruction by the Chilean army in 1881 and which the Brothers Backer regarded as lost. "La Vida de V. P. Diego Alvarez de Paz," which Father Arriaga was taking to Spain to be printed and which, according to Father Barraza, was lost by the death of the author on board the ship that was taking him to the Peninsula.

In the year 1622 the Provincial of the Society, Father Juan de Frías Herrán, needed to communicate to the general of the order in Rome certain matters of an urgent character which could not wait upon the meeting of the Provincial Congregation to take place in 1624. This was with regard to the election of procurators and "was the occasion," says Father Nieremberg, "when some business of lofty import and great consideration such as the founding of new schools and other matters in which the good name of the Society was deeply involved were to come before the province. As both matters depended on His Majesty the King and his Royal Council of the Indies, it was deemed necessary to dispatch a member of our Society to court, a man of parts and altogether satisfactory for the success of our affairs." For this mission the Provincial chose Father Arriaga who, when asked if he were ready to go, replied that he could go at once. Two days later Father Arriaga embarked at Callao for Panama, accompanied by Father Claudio Celini, who had been given permission to return to his province. The voyage on the Pacific was entirely successful, and a few days after leaving Callao the fleet reached Panama. From this city the Father went to Portobello, where he embarked for Havana to change there to a fleet which was leaving for the Peninsula. This squadron consisted of twenty-eight vessels. It had barely cleared the port when it was surprised by a violent storm that caused the loss of four galleons, with the millions of pesos which they were carrying to Spain. According to Saldamando, *Los antiguos Jesuitas del Perú,* and Medina, *La imprenta en Lima,* it was on approaching Havana that the storm overtook the fleet, but Father Nieremberg affirms that it occurred "when the galleons and ships were just leaving Havana and had barely cleared the port." Father Arriaga died on board the ship in which he was traveling during the storm, as the letters of several eyewitnesses tell. One of these letters is from Father Friar Pedro Puerto of the Jeronimite Order, a great friend of Father Arriaga, who was on the ship with him. It is addressed to the rector of the Colegio de San Martín, and it says:

In the midst of my affliction and sorrow, not the least of my worries was anxiety as to whether Father Joseph was in one of the four ships that had been lost to sight. I reached Havana and learned that he had suffered adverse fortune. I sought out Don Bernardino de Lugo, Knight of the Habit of Malta, and captain of the galleon's infantry, who, with some sailors, had escaped. When I asked him about Father Joseph and Father Celini, his companion, he replied as follows:

Father Pablo Joseph, of the Society of Jesus, was in my galleon, the Santa Margarita, quartered aft with his companion, Father Claudio, and other passengers coming from Lima. Father, I should like to tell you a long story about the blessed father, but let me say briefly that among his many gifts was that of prophecy. I am alive today because of something he said. When the galleon seemed lost and grounded I made my confession to him, and absolving me he said that I could confess later at my leisure, giving me to understand that I was not going to drown. Trusting in his word I struggled to find a plank on which I might escape with my life. The Lord furnished me with it and I escaped, not knowing how to swim but trusting, as I say, in the protection of the saintly man. I had the good fortune to be rescued by a ship which happened to see me in the water, and by it I was brought to this city. Of Father Joseph's death I can say this, that he was not drowned. He stood close to a longboat holding in his arms the crucifix with which he had encouraged the people in the galleon and had urged them to die like good Christians. After hearing their confession he went toward a cabin, dressed in his cassock and serge cape, and there upon his knees, his eyes fixed upon the Christ that he held in his arms, he gave his soul to God. He was untouched by the torment that afflicted everyone else. This boon Our Lord granted him for his saintliness and virtue. All the rest were drowned except for a few sailors whom the Lord spared so that they might be witnesses of the event. I have talked to them all as such and they all agree with what the captain said, and thus I have written it down.

The Provincial of the Society of Jesus in the kingdom of New Granada in a letter to the Provincial of the province of Peru refers to the death of Father Arriaga as having occurred on Tuesday, September 6, 1622, at six o'clock in the morning during the terrible storm.

His letter is as follows:

The sad news of the storm and the loss of the galleons and the ships of the fleet has touched this kingdom, and I am certain that it will touch the other since both provinces share in it. We have felt particular grief in the loss and death of Father Joseph and his companion. We are not alone in this sentiment, as the secular priests also weep for the death of our good (and as they say) sainted Father Joseph, which occurred after he had been two days ceaselessly preaching and confessing, down on his knees, embracing a crucifix before the galleon went down. When they reached him, he was found to have expired, and when the sailors saw this they said that if Father Joseph was dead they were all lost, and then they went to the bottom. The case of the captain, who risked the same fate as the rest, was a curious one, since Father Joseph had prophesied that he would not drown. He advised him to make his confession later, at his leisure, and so it turned out. The feelings here are deep on account of the death of our good father, and such is his reputation for saintliness that people say that the greatest loss, after that of so many galleons, is that of Father Joseph.

In Havana solemn funerals were celebrated for all the religious who perished during this terrible storm, and in the part of the tomb that was given over to Father Arriaga the following epitaph was placed:

Here lies the servant of Jesus Christ, the very Christian Father Joseph de Arriaga.

According to Father Nieremberg, Father Arriaga was "of short stature, something less than average in height, round-faced, with hidden cheekbones, a scanty beard, grayish in color, and a venerable appearance, who breathed the devotion and sanctity which were undoubtedly great in this holy man." The same biographer says that Father Arriaga died at the age of sixty along with forty-five members of the Society of Jesus, of whom thirty-seven were from the province of Peru.

We do not know what rude hand tore out of the unpublished work of Father Anello Oliva's "Historia del Perú y varones insignes en santidad de la Compañía de Iesus," preserved in the National Library of this city, the pages corresponding to the biographies of Fathers Arriaga and Menacho. The manuscript fortunately came into the possession of Felipe Alegambe, who published an extract from it in his *Bibliotheca scriptoribus Societas Iesu,* printed in Madrid in 1644. Thus the damage done to the original manuscript can be remedied in part. It should also be noted that the library has acquired the Oliva manuscript with this mutilation in its interesting pages.

Father Friar Buenaventura de Salinas y Córdoba gave enthusiastic praise to Father Arriaga in his *Memorial de las historias del Nuevo Mundo,* printed in Lima in 1630.

The *americanista,* Clement R. Markham, has some harsh words for Father Arriaga for destroying the idols of the Indians, but he did not take into account the spirit of the times and the mission of Father Arriaga with its religious character. For us the accusation is unfair. No purpose would have been served by preserving the stones and other objects of the cult of the ancient Peruvians if there had not existed a minute account of the value and significance of these objects among the Indians. For this the work of Father Arriaga is invaluable.

Lima, *1919*   Carlos A. Romero

THE EXTIRPATION
OF IDOLATRY
IN PERU

TO THE KING OUR LORD

IN HIS ROYAL COUNCIL OF THE INDIES

SIR: The love which all your vassals bear Your Majesty and their desire to serve you in every way has awakened in the minds of many of them a desire to find new plans and new means of increasing your royal income in this new world. In the year 1602, while Your Majesty was in Valladolid, I was in Rome whither I had been sent from Lima by order of my superiors, and I learned of two persons who had gone forth from this kingdom of Peru who had given Spain the expectation of a means of increasing the royal treasury by some millions. Another had a plan for establishing a salt monopoly, which is like putting doors on the countryside, for there is as great an abundance of it here as of earth and water. Another, with a priest's good intentions, carried hence a plan for the establishment of a gambling house in each city, thus setting up a playing-card monopoly. All these plans and three or four others were formed in that year and proposals in their behalf were made. All were listened to and then dismissed like so much fairy treasure, salt in the sea, or frivolous matters. My plan is to save souls held in the cruel slavery of the Devil, and to increase our Christian faith and religion in this kingdom. This is the true treasure sought by Your Majesty, through which and for which Our Lord adds unto us so much of the gold, silver, and pearls of this kingdom. The boon I ask for serving Your Majesty is this: that you hear me. For I am certain that because of the great zeal for the increase of the Catholic faith which burns in your bosom which you have inherited from your ancestors, you will order proper steps to be taken in a matter of such great service to Our Lord and for the good of the royal crown. So that after many long and happy years you may live in eternal glory, as we all pray and supplicate the Divine Majesty.

Of Your Royal and Christian Majesty, I am
your unworthy and humblest servant,
Pablo Joseph de Arriaga

PREFACE

To the Reader

WHILE I was engaged in a visit for the extirpation of idolatry with two fathers of our Society and with Dr. Avendaño, at present a priest of the Metropolitan Church in this city, I wrote this account. The curious nature of the things I saw provided its beginning, the utility that might be implied for the future insured its continuance, the necessity for a remedy for so great an evil as is being discovered led to its conclusion. I did not intend to write a history, although a long and varied one could be written of the antiquities, fables, rites, and ceremonies which the Indians of this kingdom have had and which they have not yet abandoned. I have simply written a brief and summary account of what is being observed. And so that the book of my failures, so to speak, may become the book of my successes, permitting the experiences of some persons to supply what is lacking to others, I read what I had written on my return from the mission to some fathers gathered together from distant places at that time in chapter, or the Provincial Congregation. I wanted to make them realize that a great deal of evil had been hidden and that there were more idolatry and pagan rites in the areas in which their reverences were traveling than had been discovered in this archbishopric. There was much argument over this, for some doubted and others disbelieved, and to treat the matter a special deputation was created. I did not wish time, which changes all truths, to change mine to that extent. The Lord Prince of Esquilache, viceroy of this kingdom, heard about my account and read it in draft form, and His Excellency thought it should be printed, though I had not written it with that intention. Father Diego Alvarez de Paz, who was then provincial of this province, gave the same order, having first read it in the presence of other fathers, but he ordered certain things deleted that might have seemed improper in print. Nevertheless, the Licentiate Cacho de Santillana, then a crown agent and now a justice of the peace in the court of His Majesty, who also read it, thought it should be printed without change. By order of the aforesaid Father Provincial, other fathers looked at it together, and by order of the present Father Provincial, Juan de Frías Herrán, another three read it. The five visitors of idolatry who are mentioned in it saw it, each by himself, especially Dr. Hernando de Avendaño, from whose papers and observations I drew much of my material. Finally by order of the Viceroy and the Archbishop it was entrusted to two other qualified persons. All agreed that it should be printed for the purpose for which it was intended, that is, to discover and remedy an evil that is very well hidden. I have said all this so that it may be known and understood that the truth has been told in its entirety. And if great care was used in the writing, the work has been looked over and revised with even greater care before printing.

Although this account is not divided into parts, it may be divided into three. The first: What idols and huacas the Indians have and what sacrifices and festivals they perform. What ministers and priests they have and what their abuses and superstitions in paganism are to this very day. Second: Why, since they are Christians, and even the sons and grandsons of Christians, this evil has not been uprooted, and what the means are of uprooting it. Third: How, in detail, visits for the extirpation of idolatry should be carried out.

This treatise will serve such a purpose. It will be useful for persons who hold the office of visitor to help them acquire some notion of the evils which require so great a remedy. By it the priests may be forewarned of the care they must exercise with those under their surveillance, of whom God will demand a strict accounting. It will show the confessors how to confess and the preachers the truths they must teach and the errors they must refute. It will show the visitors how to fulfill their obligation, and, what is most important, it will satisfy grave and learned persons who have not only doubted what is herein clearly proved, but who have declared on many occasions that there is no idolatry among the Indians, but that they are all good Christians. As if in less than ninety years, since the Gospel began to be preached in these parts, more could have been accomplished, and by ministers superior to those in Spain, than was accomplished there in six hundred years. For the Gospel was preached there by sainted prelates and doctors and watered with the blood of famous martyrs, yet even so idolatry raised its head and could not be cut down. In order that the same care may be taken as was taken by those sainted fathers, and that those who have similar responsibilities may learn from them, I shall quote from the canons of the Third National Council of Toledo, where, by the King's preference, the Archbishop of Seville, Bishop San Leandro, brother of San Ermenegildo, was present, in the year of Our Lord 589. Chapter 12 is as follows:

Quoniam poene per omnem Hispaniam Idolatriae sacrilegium inolevit, hoc cum consensu gloriossisimi Principis sancta Synodus ordinavit, ut omnis Sacerdos in loco suo una cum Iudice territorii, sacrilegium memoratum studiose perquirat, et exterminare inventum non differat: homines vero qui ad talem errorem concurrunt, salvo, discrimine animae, qua potuerint animadversione coerceant. Quod si neglexerint, sciant se utique excommunicationis periculum esse subituros. Si qui vero Domini extirpare hoc malum a possessione sua neglexerint, vel familiae suae prohibere noluerint ab Episcopo, et ipsi a communione pellantur.

The same thing was commanded in the eleventh chapter of the Twelfth Council of Toledo in the year 681 and in the Sixteenth Council of Toledo in the year 693, in the second chapter where, among other things, it says:

Si qui vero pro tali defensione obstiterint, Sacerdotibus, aut iudicibus, ea nec emendent ut debet, nec extirpent, ut condecet, et non potius cum eis exquisitores, ultores, seu extirpatores tanti criminis extiterint, sint Anathema in conspectu individuae Trinitatis: et in super, si nobilis persona fuerit, auri libras tres sacratiissimo

Fisco exolvat: si inferior centenis verberibus flagellabitur ac turpiter decalvabitur, medietas rerum suarum Fisci vivibus applicabitur.

A council can hardly be cited in which this point has not been discussed as one of the most important for the increase of the Catholic religion. In all that I have written I have tried not to offend nor to flatter anyone, but to serve and profit all. Let my good will be acceptable and with it pardon my faults.

Farewell

CHAPTER ONE

How Idolatry Came to Be Discovered
in the Archbishopric of Lima

ALTHOUGH the Indians of Peru have been Christians for years, it is well known that some traces of idolatry still persist in all their towns and provinces. Nor will it be marveled at that so ancient an evil, and one so deeply ingrained and natural to the Indians, should not have been completely eradicated. Anyone who has studied the ecclesiastical histories from the beginning, as well as the evolution of the church, and who understands what has happened in our Spain can see that the Jews are outsiders there still despite the fact that they came to the country more than 1,500 years ago, in the time of the Emperor Claudius. For it has scarcely been possible to extirpate so evil a seed even in so clean a land, where the Gospel has been so continuously, so carefully, and so thoroughly preached and where the Most Righteous Tribunal of the Holy Office has been so diligently and solicitously vigilant.

The problem of setting aright and causing to be forgotten errors of belief learned at a mother's breast and inherited from father to son can readily be seen in the recent example we have had before us in the expulsion of the Moors from Spain. For they were provided with every possible remedy for their evils without effecting their true conversion, as intended, and, since the disease was more powerful than the medicine and there was no hope of spiritual remedy, it became necessary as with misguided folk to avoid the temporal damage that was feared and to expel them from the country. The disease of our Indians is not so deeply rooted a cancer. The remedy is easy for those who wish to be cured, as they do when their disease is pointed out to them. What is needed is a cure, or cures, and the realization that the evil is worse than was supposed. For in the beginning no one believed in its existence, and even now there are those who, because they cannot see it or touch it with their hands, are skeptical and refuse to believe in it at all.

The first person to discover this evil, which was so well hidden, to deduce, as they say, the presence of the hank from the piece of yarn, was Dr. Francisco de Avila when he was a priest at the mission of San Damián, in the province of Huarochirí.[1] While he was preaching, as he always did, with the good talent the Lord had given him, he began to flush game, for the Divine Goodness was not willing that *verbum suum semper revertatur vacuum.* When he had ascertained the presence of certain superstitions among the Indians, he punished them publicly. Then he reproached them and spoke out against idolatry, helping them to understand by the example of some saints, martyred in testimony of their faith, who for refusing to worship idols or huacas had suffered many torments and lost their earthly life in order to reach the eternal, which they now enjoy in great glory. After this sermon an Indian came up and said to him:

"Father, in a certain place an Indian martyr lies buried under an overhanging rock. It seems that the Indians of a certain clan and faction were sacrificing to a huaca, and when this Indian happened to pass by they invited him to their festival. Not only did he refuse, but because they were Christians he reproached them severely for what they were doing. Then he continued on his way."

Then the Indians, either because they were irritated at

---

[1] This diligent and learned priest, while exercising the curacy of San Damián in the province of Huarochirí, worked enthusiastically to extirpate idolatry, and this caused complaints from the Indians and recriminations which reached the archbishop of Lima. The Reverend Avila was obliged to prepare a brief report in his defense. Having obtained his vindication, he requested a new curacy, which was accorded him. He was named priest of Huánuco by a royal decree, dated 1610. Relating to this enlightened priest, see the lengthy biography of Don José Toribio Polo, in this collection [Colección de libros y documentos referentes a la historia del Perú, edited by Horacio H. Urteaga; hereafter cited as Colección Urteaga, First Series, I, xv-xxxii].

what he had said or feared his telling other people about them, went after him and killed him and buried him where the Indian said. Dr. Avila removed the body and buried it in the church in Santiago de Tumna[2] at the foot of the high altar, close to the altar hanging. His name was Indian Martin, and this was an indication, the first among many, that revealed the existence of idolatry. But this was contrary to the common opinion, and those who by reason of their office and obligation should have encouraged Dr. Avila paid no attention to his suggestions. Still he went on working, little by little, persisting in his efforts until he discovered the truth, or discovered (perhaps we should say) the error, and the extent of idolatry among the Indians became known. He found more than six hundred idols, many of them with their ornaments, garments, and shawls made of *cumbi*.[a] These shawls ill befitted the idols, most of which were of stone, of various shapes, and fairly modest in size. But one should not be astonished to hear that the Indians recognize deity in small things, for it is known that these figures and stones are images representing hills, mountains, and river beds, or even their progenitors and forebears, whom they invoke and worship as their creators and from whom they expect well-being and happiness. I mean temporal and visible happiness, since of the spiritual and eternal they have little or no appreciation. Nor do they commonly hope for it or ask for it. Since even after seeing the idols the Marqués de Montes-Claros, viceroy of this kingdom,[3] was still skeptical and not persuaded that the homage and veneration that the Indians gave them was idolatry, Dr. Francisco de Avila told the story of each idol and its history and fable (for the Indians have long and numerous stories about their huacas). Finally, in a meeting of grave and learned

[2] Tumna should read Tuna, in the *corregidor* district of Huarochirí. Alcedo, *Diccionario geográfico,* IV, 232.

[3] The Marqués de Montes-Claros, the eleventh viceroy of Peru, governed from Dec. 21, 1607, to Dec. 18, 1615.

[a] *Cumbi* is footnoted on p. 11 of the Spanish text as fine, delicate, exquisite cloth. *Infra,* p. 16, n. 11.

persons he persuaded the Viceroy that Indian idolatry was as deepseated as it was hidden.[4]

There was a public burning of these idols in the plaza of the city of Lima, and to witness it the Indians from four leagues around were called together. Two platforms were built with a passage leading from one to the other. One was a sort of mound and on it was a pile of wood, where the idols were. The ornaments of the idols were also thrown on the woodpile, and an Indian named Hernando Páucar, a native of San Pedro de Mama[5] and a great master of idolatry, who talked to the Devil, was tied to the stake there. And this Indian was held in respect by all the Indians of his region. After Dr. Avila had preached at this execution in the general language of the Indians, the Viceroy being present and looking out of his window from which he could see and hear everything, the sentence was published, the Indian was whipped, and they set fire to the wood around the idols. Don Hierónymo de Avellaneda, *corregidor* of the Indians of this city and its surroundings, took upon himself the labor of organizing this execution. With him worked Don Fernando de Córdoba, the civil mayor, and these two led Dr. Avila out of his house with much pomp.

With all this effort some persons began to be persuaded of the existence of idolatry among the Indians, and if doubts still remained among the skeptical, they disappeared upon the arrival of the fathers of our Society[b] who came to aid Dr. Avila in his glorious enterprise. To demonstrate the truth of matters in which so many persons still found grounds for doubt, six fathers of our Society, among the oldest and most experienced in Indian affairs, were to be sent to various places at various times. Among them was Father Gaspar de Montalvo, who

[4] The aforesaid account, enlarged by Dr. Avila, was published in 1608 and is reproduced in Colección Urteaga, First Series, XI, 57-132.

[5] San Pedro de Mama, a town in the present province of Huarochirí, near the mission of San Juan de Matucana.

[b] In Spanish the Jesuits are generally referred to as La Compañía de Jesús. In English, Society of Jesus is the usual term.

died during the investigation. All of them came back saying: *sicut audivimus sic vidimus,* that the evil was more extensive than had been reported, and that it would require an appropriate and efficacious remedy. Such a remedy began to be applied by order of the Viceroy, the Marqués de Montes-Claros, and the Lord Archbishop, Don Bartolomé Lobo Guerrero,[6] whom Our Lord sent at this time to this church to uproot from his archbishopric the deep and prejudicial roots of idolatry. Both of these persons, as princes zealous of the glory of God, gave the necessary instructions and authority to Dr. Francisco de Avila for a visit to the province of Huarochirí for this purpose. They also sent fathers of our Society to catechize, preach, and confess in the towns that were visited. After the province of Huarochirí, Dr. Avila visited that of Yauyos, whose missions are in the hands of the Dominican fathers. He went in the company of Father Friar Juan de Mercado, of that same holy order of preachers, a man learned in theology, experienced in Indian affairs, and a great preacher in their language as well as in Spanish. He also visited a large part of the province of Xauxa, discovered and burned many huacas, and found so much idolatry and so many ministers thereof that with the fame of his reforms many eyes began to be opened and the priests of the Indian towns began to notice what they had not noticed before. When he had made inquiries and learned the facts about idolatry he communicated them to His Illustrious Lordship, who sent out special commissions of inquiry.

In the beginning the hardest aspect of discovering idolatrous practices came from the resistance of the Indians, from the opposition of Spaniards and Indians, the Indians' refusal to reveal them, and from everyone else for not believing that they existed. Dr. Avila found much idolatry in the province of Yauyos, especially in the town of Visca, and a great many ministers of idolatry, but he encountered much difficulty in finding them out because no one believed in their existence.

[6] Don Bartolomé Lobo Guerrero was the third archbishop of Lima and ruled his extensive diocese from 1609 to 1622.

For what the Indians revealed to the visitor alone and in private they denied in public, until finally Dr. Avila, who was no less sagacious than industrious, painstaking, and effective, secretly placed two trustworthy Spaniards behind the bed in his room to listen to what the Indians would admit privately, especially the *caciques*,[c] who most insistently made denial in public. Therefore, the Lord Archbishop, having learned in this way about the difficulties and contradictions encountered by Dr. Avila, sent out Dr. Diego Ramírez, a priest then located in the parish of Santa Ana de Lima,[7] since he was learned in theology, a good speaker, and much experienced in Indian affairs, to inform himself of the truth. And when proof of idolatry was discovered, he was to help him to make a record of it. He did this, and after they had traveled together for some time, with the information that he already had and the commission that His Illustrious Lordship had given him, he went to visit twelve towns in the province of Huarochirí, and in them discovered no fewer things than had Dr. Avila in the towns of Yauyos. With this information Dr. Diego Ramírez returned to Lima, and going to the Lord Viceroy and Lord Archbishop, who were prone to disbelieve and contradict him, he gave public testimony about the matter in the cathedral in their presence and in that of all the King's audience, charging them to do their duty by providing a remedy for so great a wrong.

After this they sent fathers to catechize, teach, and confess in the towns already visited. And soon the aforesaid Dr. Diego Ramírez set out again with new authority and a commission to visit the provinces of Tarama and Chinchacocha[8]

---

[7] This parish exists to this very day, but with the increase in the size of the city it has been subdivided into five vice-parishes. Archepiscopal decree of July 19, 1919.

[8] Read Tarma and Chinchaycocha, by which names they are known today.

[c] The word *cacique* was learned by the Spaniards in the Caribbean area and then used throughout Latin America as a synonym for the Spanish *jefe*. The Quechua word is *curaca*. Both words occur in this book and are used as synonyms by writers of the period.

in the company of some fathers of our Society, among whom was Father Benito de Arroyo, who died in the town of San Miguel de Ullucmáyoc. The profit derived from this activity was very great and would take a long time to tell. One thing I must not fail to mention is that while Dr. Diego Ramírez was in the town of Ninacaca, where because of the intolerable cold he had to stay close to the fire, he was privately examining a minister of idolatry one day. He had purposely ordered a young child to stay with him and stir up the fire, thinking the child would not notice what was being said and that the Indian would not hesitate to answer in his presence. As the visitor was asking about the huacas of the town, about which he had some information, the Indian stubbornly refused to talk. Suddenly the boy, without being spoken to, said to the old man:

"What do you deny this and that?"

The boy then told about the idol that was being asked about, where it was and the sacrifices offered to it, and said that the man there present was its minister. After this the adult Indian began to reveal the idolatry of the town and to tell all about it. This case was thought to be, if not a miracle, at least a marvelous occurrence. Among the rest of the Indians was one who had gone on a pilgrimage of more than thirty leagues, visiting the principal huacas and places of worship in Peru, and he even went as far as Mollo Ponco, which is at the entrance to Potosí, a place very famous among the Indians.

After the aforementioned visitors, the next to give attention to the matter was Dr. Hernando de Avendaño, who was then serving the mission of San Pedro de Casta in that same province of Huarochirí. In that area by a special commission from the Lord Archbishop, he visited a few towns. Some time later, while he was priest and vicar in the province of Checras,[9] he visited still other towns and discovered in them much idolatry and many huacas, among them one famous among the Indians and venerated even in remote villages. This was the

[9] Chacras. This name is applied to a very cold mountain region in the province of Chancay. See Alcedo, *Diccionario geográfico*, I, 463.

mummy of a very ancient *curaca,* named Libiacancharco, located about a league and a half from the town of San Cristóbal de Rapaz in a shelter below a cave in a very steep mountain. It had its *huama,*[10] or diadem of gold, on its head and was dressed in seven fine shirts of cumbi.[11] These, the Indians said, had been sent to them as a present by the ancient Inca kings. This mummy, and that of a majordomo of his called Chuchu Michuy, located in a different place and much venerated by the Indians, were brought to Lima just as they were for the Lord Viceroy and the Lord Archbishop to see. They were paraded publicly and then a solemn auto-da-fé was held to which all the inhabitants of the province were invited, and the mummies were burned together with a great many huacas, to the great consternation and fear of the Indians. For up to that time the Indians had never seen Libiacancharco, though they had venerated him, worshiped him, and feared him by name alone, according to the tradition of their ancestors. Everywhere many huacas were found, and their ministers and the Indians were reconciled to the church, taught, and confessed.

In such a state did the Marqués de Montes-Claros leave the remedy for the evil of idolatry, and when the Prince of Esquilache came to this kingdom he was informed by many persons, especially by Dr. Alberto de Acuña, a member of the Royal Audience of Lima, of the need for continuing what had been begun and for adopting the most efficacious means of uprooting idolatry among the Indians. As soon as His Excellency could free himself of his first obligations in the government, he set up a most promising consultation with the most serious-minded persons, ecclesiastical and secular, sending them notice of it several days in advance.

At this meeting it was agreed, among the many remedies

[10] *Huama* should read *huaman,* which means falcon or totem of the Indians of the Peruvian coast. The latter had the custom of adorning their foreheads with straps on which were drawn the figure of the sacred bird. [Father Arriaga uses *huama,* and the translator has followed suit.]
[11] *Cumbi.* Fine, delicate, exquisite cloth.

proposed, that in the Cercado de Lima a house should be established, which came to be called the house of Santa Cruz. There all the dogmatizers and ministers of idolatry should be confined, and since not all of them could be assembled there, one should be chosen from each town in order to frighten the rest. A boarding school should be set up for the sons of the caciques, for as they afterward became so would all the Indians be; and visitors*d* should be dispatched to various parts of the kingdom with friars to aid and abet them. For this task Dr. Francisco de Avila, who was in his benefice in the city of Huánuco, Dr. Diego Ramírez, of the mission of Santa Ana, and Dr. Hernando de Avendaño, vicar of Collana de Lampas, were chosen. After they had come to Lima, those who had not been present at the previous meeting conferred several times among themselves as to the manner of conducting a visit. The Lord Archbishop had divided them among the three provinces of his archbishopric, and on his behalf and on behalf of the Viceroy, they were given financial aid as well as the instructions and authority necessary for the performance of their task. His Excellency gave the six fathers of our Society who were appointed to accompany them all the necessary supplies, liberally and in full measure. Dr. Avila, to whom Huamalíes, Conchucos,[12] and Huánuco had been assigned, with all the surrounding region, was unable for reasons of ill health to begin his visit as soon as the rest. He had to turn back in Chaupiguarangas, only three days' journey from Huánuco. Dr. Diego Ramírez, with three of the friars, set out to visit the province of Huaylas in February of last year, 1617. At the same time Dr. Hernando de Avendaño set out with the other three friars for a visit which began with the town of San Bartolomé de Huacho, in the *corregidor* district of Chancay. I was to be among this last group, although His Excellency

[12] Conchucos, in the provinces of Huaylas and Huarás, department of Ancash.

d As the context will plainly show, these persons were actually investigators or inspectors. The words *visit* and *visitor* are used by Father Arriaga both in the usual sense and in this special sense.

was keeping me busy setting up the school for the caciques' sons and building the house of Santa Cruz. But he ordered me to set out on this visit, and so I left both tasks in progress and in charge of another friar. I accompanied Dr. Avendaño for a year and a half, and Dr. Francisco de Avila for some months. Thus, whatever I have to say will be either as an eye-witness or as one informed by persons of as much authority as my own, or even more.

With the greater authority and control obtained both from His Excellency and from the Archbishop, with the experience obtained from previous visits, and by acting more decisively and opportunely than before, the visitors discovered so many cases of idolatry and paganism that it became evident that all the provinces and Indian towns of the archbishopric were as bad if not worse than those visited in previous years in Huarochirí, Yauyos, Xauxas, Andajes, and Chinchacochas. It was therefore quite necessary to revisit the provinces already visited, as they had been instructed to do.

Huacas belonging to persons and clans were found everywhere, with their fiestas, their sacrifices, and offerings. There were major and minor priests for sacrifices and various officials for the several kinds of ministry, and they practiced many abuses, superstitions, and traditions of their ancestors. But what caused us most sorrow was their supreme ignorance of the mysteries and concerns of our faith, and this was the heart of the matter. From this ignorance stems the little or no esteem in which they hold divine worship and the ceremonies and intercession of the church. In many places, in fact wherever they have managed to do so, they have removed the bodies of their dead from the church and taken them out to the fields to their *machays*,[13] or burial places of their ancestors. The reason they give for this is expressed by the word *cuyaspa*, or the love they bear them. In conclusion, to demonstrate their wretched condition, their extreme need for a remedy,

[13] *Machay* is a cave, den, or cavern to rest in and also, more specifically, a closet or vaulted niche which the Indians fashion in the rock for the mummies or funeral offerings to the dead.

and the ease with which they receive it, no proof is needed beside that of seeing them on one of their exhibition days, when they bring out all the accessories of their idolatry. They are grouped about the plaza by clans and factions and bring out the mummified bodies of their ancestors, called *munaos*[14] in the lowlands and *malquis*[15] in the sierra, together with the bodies taken from the church, and it looks like the living and the dead come to judgment. They also bring out their personal huacas, and the more eminent ministers bring out the huacas that are worshiped in common. Offerings are prepared for them and they display the garments used in the festivals and the plumage in which they deck themselves; the pots, jugs, and tumblers used to make and drink *chicha* and offer it to the huacas; the trumpets, usually of copper although sometimes of silver, and the great horns and other instruments[e] by which they are summoned to a festival. There are also a great many well-made drums of small size, for nearly every woman brings her own for the songs and dances. The towns of the lowlands have their elaborate cradles, their antlers and horns of mountain goats,[16] their fox skins and lion pelts, and many other things of the sort, which have to be seen to be believed.

When the visitor examines an Indian privately he writes down what he tells him about these things, and at the same time, by his order, they exhibit what they claim to possess. Everything that is inflammable is burned at once and the rest is broken in pieces. If we were to tell what resulted in the province of Huaylas, we could make a long and sorrowful history. Dr. Ramírez had visited there in years past, and the licentiate Juan Delgado, then the priest of Huarás in the same province, visited it again. We could also relate what happened

[14] *Munaos.* See Calancha, *Crónica moralizada de la Orden de San Agustín,* Vol. I, Bk. II, Chaps. IX and X.

[15] *Malquis.* See *ibid. Malquis* also means a plant.

[16] *Taruga.* Garcilaso calls them *taruca. Comentarios reales,* Pt. I, Bk. VIII, Chap. XVII, p. 361 (Horacio Urteaga, Colección de historiadores clásicos del Perú, Vol. II).

[e] The chief instruments of the Incas were horns, flutes, and drums. See Robert Stevenson, *The Music of Peru* (Washington: Pan-American Union, 1959).

in Conchucos and the many other towns that he visited, and what the Licentiate Luis de Aguilar found in towns of the sierra, and what Dr. Alonso Osorio found there, and what Dr. Avendaño found in the mountains as well as in the lowlands in the *corregidor* districts of Chancay and Cajatambo, and it would make a long and sorrowful story. But I shall summarize briefly, speaking as an eye-witness of the huacas,[17] sorcerers, *conopas,* and other instruments of idolatry which were found in the towns visited by Dr. Hernando de Avendaño in the year and a half that I accompanied him. I could even list in detail what was found in each town, though the towns are not mentioned by name (a fact much deplored by the Indians). Nevertheless, I shall merely summarize the most important details regarding each town as it appeared in the first visit, which occurred last year between February 1617 and July 1618. There were 5,694 confessions; 669 ministers of idolatry were discovered and punished; 603 principal huacas were taken away from them, as well as 3,418 conopas,[18][f] 45 *mamazaras,*[19] 189 *huancas*[g] (which are different from huacas), and 617 *malquis;* 63 witches of the lowlands were punished. About 357 cradles were burned, 477 bodies were returned to the church, not counting many bodies of *chacpas*[20] and

---

[17] *Huaca,* according to Garcilaso, signifies an idol in its first meaning, but it is also equivalent to a sacred object and is then applied to crags, stones, trees, offerings, etc. See *Comentarios reales,* Bk. II, Chaps. IV and V (Colección de historiadores, Vol. I); *huaca,* idol or temple. It is also used for treasure. Cieza de León, *Crónica general del Perú,* Chap. XXI.

[18] *Conopas.* Calancha, *Crónica moralizada,* Vol. I, Bk. II, p. 367. Villagómez, *Exhortación contra las idolatrías,* Colección Urteaga, XII, 206.

[19] *Mamazara* means mother of the corn; they were ears of rare shape which had a beautiful appearance, or several ears joined together. Many of these forms were reproduced by the potters and are exhibited in museums. The private museum of Dr. Javier Prado in Lima has several examples. See Villagómez, Colección Urteaga, Vol. XII, Chap. L, p. 208. Calancha, *Crónica moralizada,* Bk. III, Chap. XI, p. 367.

[20] *Chacpa* is a child born feet first. He was regarded by the Indians as a privileged being. He was generally dedicated to sorcery or the priesthood, and when he died his mummy was venerated.

[f] Cf. pp. 28-30.

[g] Father Arriaga defines this word as a large stone placed in front of a house to protect it. Cf. p. 30.

chuchus,[21] which are also venerated and kept in the house, without mentioning the *pactos*,[22] *axomamas*,[23] *micsazara*,[24] *huantayzara*,[25] *huayriguazara*,[26] and the thousand other things they are superstitious about. All these things we burned, as we shall explain in the following chapters. Thirty-one towns, some of them rather small, contained such objects, and four of them had been visited three years before by their priest, Don Plácido Antolínez, holding a special commission from the Lord Archbishop. He found out and burned many huacas and conopas, although quite a few remained hidden. In general, we could observe much improvement in the town since the first visit, though there were no few cases of backsliding, especially among the sorcerers. The most guilty of these was the first man to be brought into the house of Santa Cruz.[27]

Great diligence was employed in these discoveries and in removing these objects from their sight. Even more particularly, we tried by continual sermons and catechisms to remove them from their hearts, but it is greatly to be feared that roots so ancient and so deep will not yield entirely to the first plowing. To make sure they are really uprooted and will not flourish again, a second and third plowing will be required. One thing is certain, that all the Indians visited have been taught and shown the error of their superstitions. And they have been warned by punishment. Therefore, their children will be better than the parents and their grandchildren better than the fathers and grandfathers. By this reasoning, the

[21] *Chuchus* means multiple birth, or twins. The term was also applied to fruit that grew double or triple. *Sarachuchu* means double or twin ears of corn.

[22] *Pactos* [*sic*], as it should read, means equal bodies or those similar in form or color.

[23] *Axomamas*, mother potato or first potato.

[24] *Michacasara*, as it should read, was the first corn that ripened.

[25] *Huantaysara* means the tallest corn, highest on the stalk.

[26] *Hayrihuasara* [*sic*] means two kernels of black and white corn growing together, or two ears from one stalk.

[27] The house of Santa Cruz del Cercado was a prison for Indian sorcerers, ordered built by the Prince of Esquilache, viceroy of Peru.

glorious Saint Gregory the Great, rightly called the apostle of England, encouraged those first saints whom he sent to that kingdom to uproot idolatry despite all difficulties. From the accomplishments of this visit one can infer what must have been done during both previous and subsequent ones. More time will be available, the towns will be more numerous, and there will be no slackening in the visitors' efforts, yet there will be as much idolatry as has been encountered up to now.

As the Lord Viceroy Don Martín Enríquez[28] has well observed, the Indians are not only several, but one.

CHAPTER TWO

What the Indians Worship Today and of What Their Idolatry Consists

MUCH COULD be said about this, and something has been written in the treatise at the end of the confession, compiled by order of the Council of Lima in the year 1582.[1] Anyone who reads it will know what the Indians formerly did, so I shall now summarize the objects of worship in the towns already visited and those now in process of visitation, for they will not differ from the objects of worship in towns yet to be visited.

In many places, especially in the sierra, they worship the sun as Punchao,[2] which means day, and also under its own name, Inti. They worship the moon, which they call Quilla, and

[28] Viceroy Don Martín Enríquez de Almanza, successor of Don Francisco de Toledo, was the sixth viceroy and governed Peru from 1581 to 1583.

[1] Published in Colección Urteaga, First Series, III.

[2] *Punchao*, lord of the day. The sun had two names, the generic name Inti and that of Punchao, equivalent to the sun in all its splendor.

some star, especially Oncoy, which represents the Pleiades.[3a]
They also worship Líbiac, or lightning, which is very common
in the mountains, and many of them take the name and surname Líbiac or Hillapa, which means the same thing.[4]

The worship of these objects is not performed every day
but at a festival time, or when they find themselves in difficulties or in sickness, or expect to take a journey. Then they raise
their hands and pull out their eyebrows and blow them
upward, talking all the while to the sun or to Líbiac, calling
it their maker and creator and asking it to help them.[5] They
invoke Mamacocha, or the sea, in the same way, and come
down from the sierra to the lowlands to call upon it. They ask
it especially to keep them from sickness and to let them return
home from their errand in health and with profit. All of them
do this, even the very small children.[6]

They also reverence the earth as Mamapacha, especially the
women at seed time. They talk to it and ask for a good harvest
and pour out chicha and corn meal, either by themselves or
through the intermediary of a sorcerer.

In the same way they worship *puquios*, or the streams and
springs, especially when water is scarce, begging them not to
dry up.

When they have to cross a river they take a little water in
their hands, and as they drink it they talk to the river, asking
it to let them cross over without being carried away. They
call this ceremony *mayuchulla*, and the fisherman do the same
thing when they go fishing.

They also worship and reverence the high hills and mountains and huge stones. They have names for them and

[3] According to Ondegardo, Colección Urteaga, First Series, III, 3.
Acosta, *Historia natural y moral de las Indias*, Vol. I, Bk. V, Chap. IV, p.
12. edition of 1894. Cabello Balboa, *Historia del Perú* (French ed.; Paris,
1840), Chap. V, p. 58.

[4] See the curious interpretations of Don Vicente Fidel López, *Les Races
ariennes du Pérou*, Pt. II, Chap. I, p. 148.

[5] Ondegardo, Colección Urteaga, III, 191, paragraph 11.

[6] *Ibid.*, Chap. I, p. 3.

[a] In Spanish, the Seven Goats.

numerous fables about their changes and metamorphoses, saying they were once men who have been changed to stone.

They call the snow-covered mountains *razu* or, by a fore-shortening of the word, *rao*, or *ritri*, all of which mean snow. And they reverence the houses of the *huaris*, or first dwellers in the land, whom they say were giants. Indeed, in some places there are bones of huge and incredible size which have to be seen to be believed. Judging by their dimension, the men must have been six times as tall as those of today.[7] They take dust from these for their illnesses, for the evil purposes of love, etc. They invoke Huari, the god of force, to help them when they build their *chácaras* or houses.

They also venerate their *pacarinas*,[8] or places of origin, and since they have no faith in nor knowledge of their origin in our first parents, Adam and Eve, they hold many mistaken beliefs about these matters. All of them, especially the heads of the clans, know their pacarinas and call them by name. This is one of the reasons why they resist the consolidation of their towns and like to live in such bad and difficult places. I have seen some of them where one had to descend about a league for water, and where one can neither go up nor down except on foot; the reason they give for living there is that this is their pacarina.

These are all huacas that they worship as gods, and since they cannot be removed from their sight because they are fixed and immobile, we must try to root them out of their hearts, showing them truth and disabusing them of error. They must be properly taught the sources of springs and rivers, how the lightning is forged in the sky, how the waters freeze, and other natural phenomena, which their teacher will have to know well.

[7] The bones of the giants, which the ancient chroniclers, especially Cieza de León (*Crónica*, Pt. I) and Gutiérrez de Santa Clara (*Historia de las guerras civiles del Perú* (Vol. III, Chap. LXVI, p. 566), mention so frequently, were nothing but the remains of ancient saurians scattered throughout the regions of America.

[8] *Pacarinas*, places of origin or source, that is, hills, rivers, lagoons, and the like.

The usual huacas are movable ones, which have been discovered in each town and taken away and burned. They are generally of stone and most times are without a face. Others have the faces of men and women, and some of these huacas they call the sons and wives of other huacas. Some have the faces of animals. All have their individual names by which they are invoked, and every child who has learned to talk knows the name of the huaca of his clan. For every clan and faction has a principal huaca and other less important ones, and sometimes members of the clan take the name of the community huaca. Some huacas are thought of as guardians or advocates of the town, and so, in addition to their own names, they are called *marca apárac* or *marcachárac*.[9]

All huacas have priests to offer sacrifices, and though the people know where they are, few have seen them, because they are kept out of sight where only the priest can talk to them and make offerings. For this reason, when the folk of the town see what they have not seen before but had worshiped and feared, they experience a feeling of wonder and disenchantment. They reverence not only the huaca itself, but also the places where they are supposed to have been found or placed, and they call these *zamana*. There also are other places from which they invoke them and these are called *cayan* and reverenced also. Many years ago, more than forty, as far as we have been able to ascertain, a Dominican friar named Francisco, or Miguel Cano, as he is called by some, of whom there is still remembrance and knowledge among the old men, traveled through the provinces burning and removing huacas, and in some places we have found the Indians worshiping either the name of the burned huaca or the parts of the huaca that would not burn. Therefore, great care must be taken to see that what is left over after burning is cast out where it cannot be seen.

In a town near the coast, a Spaniard threw deep into the sea four bagfuls of these accursed relics without the Indians'

[9] The defenders or guardians of the region or district.

knowing about it, and in other coast towns the same thing has been done. Elsewhere, they throw them into the river without being observed. But one must be very careful about this, scattering them, burying them, or covering them up where the Indians will not see them or know their whereabouts. This takes a great deal of trouble, for one can trust no Indian to do it, however good and reliable he may be. It is well known, for instance, that the Indians of Huaylas, although a long way away, worshiped on a bridge in Lima because some huacas that Francisco Cano had taken away from them had been thrown into the river there.

In Cahuana and Tauca, in the province of Conchucos, the visitor, Licentiate Juan Delgado, heard of a famous idol named Catequilla.[10] According to tradition, this idol was partly of gold and for that reason it was much venerated and feared throughout the province and in the province of Huamachuco, in the bishopric of Trujillo, where it had its origin, as follows: Topo Inca, the father of Huascar, was passing through with his army on his way to punish a brother who had rebelled against him in Quito. He consulted the idol Catequilla through its priests as to whether he would return victorious from the battle or die in it, and the demon in the idol answered that he would die, as indeed happened. The huaca thus acquired such a reputation that people came from remote provinces to consult it and offer it sacrifices. As a

[10] Concerning the idol Catequilla there is a great deal of information. It represented lightning and thunder and had an extensive cult in the north of Peru. Probably it was this Catequil or Catequilla to whom was dedicated the hymn of which Garcilaso has preserved the magnificent poetic passage beginning:

> Cumay ñusta
> Torallayquim
> Puñuy quita
> Paquin Cayan, etc.

See Garcilaso, *Comentarios reales*, Bk. II, Chap. XXVII. Molina, *Fábulas y ritos de los incas*, Colección Urteaga, I, 26. Acosta, *Historia*, Vol. I, Bk. V, Chap. IV. *Relación de los primeros agustinos sobre las idolatrías de los indios de Huamachuco*, Colección Urteaga, XI, 20 ff. Pedro Sarmiento de Gamboa, *Historia Indica*, paragraph 61, and for the interpretation of the myth of Catequil, see Rialle, *Mythologie comparée*, Chap. XVI, p. 259.

result, the idol became so rich that a sumptuous temple[11] was built for it. Later, when Huascar Inca, the son of Topo Inca, was passing by he noticed the magnificence of the temple, and knowing that it was this huaca which had foretold his father's death, he ordered the temple set on fire with everything in it. When the fire had started, the sorcerers and priests of the idol absconded with it to Cahuana, where they built it another temple and offered it many gifts, especially mantles and shirts of cumbi. Father Francisco Cano, whose reputation is still remembered in those provinces, discovered and destroyed all these things. It is said, however, that the Indians of the town of Tauca hid away the idol; although a diligent search has been made for it, the old men of Tauca have denied its existence, and for so doing the most guilty were sent to the house of Santa Cruz.

In this same town of Tauca they worshiped spirits called *huaraclla,* who make their appearance or cause their voices to be heard in a clump of alder trees close to town. To these spirits they dedicated maidens whose duty it was to offer them sacrifices.

Next to the stone huacas, their greatest veneration is for their malquis,[12] called in the lowlands, munaos.[13] These are the bones or mummies of their pagan ancestors, which they call the sons of the huacas; they are kept in remote fields or in their machays,[14] the latter being their ancient places of burial. Sometimes these mummies are decked out in costly shirts, or feathers of various colors, or in cumbi. The malquis have their own priests and ministers, and they celebrate for them the same festivals that are observed for the huacas. They leave with them the utensils they used during their lifetime. The women have their spindles and skeins of spun cotton, the

[11] The temple of Catequilla can still be seen, mingled with the ruins of Marca Huamachuco. See Wiener, *Pérou et Bolivie,* Chap. VIII, pp. 143-57. Similarly, *Las Informaciones de los primeros agustinos sobre las idolatrías de los indios de Huamachuco,* Colección Urteaga, XI, 18 ff.
[12] *Supra,* p. 19, n. 15.
[13] *Supra,* p. 19, n. 14.
[14] *Supra,* p. 18, n. 13.

men their *tacllas* or hoes to work the fields, or the weapons they used in war. In one of these machays of the malquis, there was a lance with an iron tip and shaft which one of the earliest of the conquerors, so they said, left to be used as a standard for the church. In another was a colorful lance called *quilcasca choque*, which means painted or carved lance. This they brought to the Viceroy. To feed these huacas and malquis, and to give them a drink, they provide utensils, sometimes gourds, sometimes vessels of clay or wood or made of silver or of seashells.

The conopas, which in Cuzco and thereabouts they call *chancas*, are really their lares and penates, or household gods. They also call them *huacicamayoc*,[15] which means majordomo, or head of the house. They are made of various materials, have a variety of faces, and are remarkable either in color or shape. It happens sometimes that they are merely peculiar little stones (of which not a few have been found), for when an Indian man or woman happens to come upon or to notice an odd-looking stone, or the like, he goes to his sorcerer and says:

"My father, I have found this. What is it?"

And he answers in great wonder:

"It is a conopa. Venerate it and worship it fervently and you will have plenty to eat, plenty of rest, and so forth."

At other times they toss about a large angular stone which serves as a die for casting lots. If the result is favorable they call it a conopa, and with this canonization the Indian acquires a household god. To illustrate the extent of their blindness and wretchedness, an Indian woman was seen wearing a piece of sealing wax. On the person of another was a little ball of silk of the sort that is used to decorate the hood of a raincape. And this is done with the notion and opinion that these things are conopas. In similar fashion another woman wore a piece of glass on the instep of her foot.

---

[15] *Huasi camayoc* means keeper or guardian of the house. The appellation *huasicamayoc* also corresponds to the porters or keepers, and even today the word *huasicama* designates in northern Peru the majordomo of those who are well off.

Conopas are usually passed on from father to son, and it has been ascertained in the towns now being visited that the eldest brother keeps the conopa of his parents and is responsible for it to his brothers and sisters. The eldest also keeps the garments for the festivals of the huacas. These are never divided among the brothers, since they are intended for divine worship. In the time of their paganism, before the Spaniards came, all the Indians certainly had conopas, just as their grandchildren have them now, for their fathers inherited them from their own fathers and never threw them away. They kept them instead as the most precious objects they had inherited. Nor, until the time of this visit, were they taken away from them.

Small sharp stones which the Indians call *quicu* are also generally regarded as conopas, and during this visit some of them have been found stained with the blood of sacrifices. In the lowlands, small pointed or angular crystals are regarded as conopas and are called *lacas.* There are also more special conopas: some for corn, called *zarap conopa,*[16] some for potatoes, called *papap conopa,*[17] and others for the increase of the herd, called *caullama,*[18] and these sometimes have the faces of sheep.

To all these conopas, of whatever sort, they accord the same worship as to huacas, except that the worship of the latter is public and common to the province, the town, or the clan according to the particular huaca, whereas the worship of conopas is secret and private for the members of a household. The cult and veneration of the conopas takes the form of personal offerings, of which we shall later speak, or of sending for some sorcerer to make the offering. In this way the sorcerer gets to know the conopas of everyone in town and can describe them.

Conopa worship does not take place every day or commonly but, as in the manner of the huacas, at certain times of the year,

[16] *Zarapconopa,* or conopa of corn, was a kind of corn totem.

[17] *Papa conopa,* or more properly, *axaconopa.*

[18] *Caullama,* a shortened form of *camayoc llama,* or more properly, according to the type of language, *llamap camayoc.*

as when the Indians are sick, or when they intend to go on a journey, or when they are about to begin their sowing.

They place a large stone high up on their houses and call it *chíchic* or huanca, and also *chacrayoc*,[19] that is, lord of the chácara, because they believe that the chácara belongs to the huaca and that he has its increase in his charge. For this reason they venerate the huaca and offer it sacrifices, especially at seed time.

Other stones of this sort, which they have in their irrigation ditches, they call *compa* or *larca villana*, and they worship them before sowing and after the water has passed by. This is to prevent the ditches from breaking and to keep water from becoming scarce.

Among the objects to be found in the towns are three kinds of *zaramamas*. The first resembles a cornhusk doll dressed like a woman. It has a mantle *(anaco)* and a shawl *(llicla)* with its silver clasp *(topo)*. They believe that this doll has a mother's power to conceive and bring forth much corn. In the same way they have *cocamamas* for the increase of coca. Others are of stone, carved like ears of corn with their kernels in relief, and they have many of these in the place of conopas. Still others are cornstalks which, because of the fertility of the soil, have produced a quantity of large ears. When two ears grow out together they call these the principal ones, or zaramamas, and venerate them as mothers of the corn. They also call them huantayzara or *ayrihuayzara*.[20] The third sort are not worshiped as huacas or conopas, but nevertheless they are regarded with superstition as sacred objects. They hang the stalks with many ears of corn from willow branches and dance with them a dance called *ayrihua*.[21] Then when the dance is over they

[19] *Chacrayoc*, a shortened form of *chacra camayoc*. It is improper to say *chácara* for a parcel of arable land or small inheritance.

[20] *Ayrihuaysara*. *Supra*, p. 21, n. 26. See also Molina, Colección Urteaga, I, 24.

[21] The *ayrihua* dances were the recreation in which they indulged after gathering the grain into *piruas* (granaries or storehouses). Thus we infer the meaning of *ayrihua* from *ayri*, corn, or ear of corn; *chuchu*, that is, two ears of corn growing from the same stalk; and *huaylli*, song, dancing song, which, with the latitude that agglutinative languages have, means

burn them and make a sacrifice to Líbiac to insure a good harvest. With the same superstition they keep brightly colored ears of corn and call them micsazara, *matayzara,*[22] or *caullazara.* Still others are called *piruazara;* these are ears whose rows of kernels are not in a straight line but in a spiral like a snail shell. The micsazara or piruazara are placed superstitiously on the piles of corn and in *piruas,* or corn cribs, to be saved. On the day of the exhibitions they bring together so many of these ears of corn that the mules have plenty to eat.

They have the same superstition about the axomamas or double potatoes, and they keep them to make sure of a good potato crop.

Human twins are called *curi,* which means two born of one womb, and if they die young they keep them in jars in the house, as a sacred object. One of them, they say, is the son of the lightning. They have many superstitions regarding the birth of twins, which we shall relate later, each of which implies some form of penance, since they must expiate the sin of having been born together.

The chacpas, or infants born feet first, are likewise kept if they die young, but if they live they add the appellation chacpas to their surname, and there is great abuse in all this. Their children, if male, are *masco,* and if female *chachi.* But the greatest abuse of all is that if they can succeed in hiding these children from the priest, they do not baptize either chuchus or chacpas.[23] During the exhibitions a great many of these chuchus and chacpas which they kept in their houses were burned.

The town cradles, already mentioned, are also huacas. They

dance and song in honor of the abundance or fecundity of the earth. D. Vicente Fidel López gives it another derivation: *"Ari,"* he says, "is the hearth; *huay* means to go toward a place, to move. The two words together mean the dance, the festival of repose." *Les Races ariennes du Pérou,* Pt. II, Chap. III, p. 188.

[22] *Micsazara* should read *michcasara,* early ripened corn, the corn most advanced in maturity; *mantaysara* [sic] should read *mantur sara,* red corn; *mantur,* red color; *caullasara* [sic], *paccho,* corn or sweet corn. *Caulla* is also bitter, dry.

[23] *Supra,* p. 20, n. 20, and p. 21, n. 21.

are fashioned like a hammock, placed on two poles at the top of which they carve faces, and called huacas. There are specially designated officials to take care of these, and when they are to be made, the relatives all gather with the official with a batch of specially prepared chicha. They all fast from salt and pepper, although they may relieve their fast by drinking. The Indian in charge of the work sprinkles chicha upon each pole as they are setting them up and speaks to the cradle. He calls it by the name of the huaca which he has bestowed upon it and adjures it to keep the child that sleeps there from crying when its mother leaves the house, to prevent anyone from harming it, etc. While thus engaged they all go on drinking.

Such are the objects which the Indians venerate, and of which their idolatry consists. Later on we shall see the kind of sacrifices they offer. Let us first see what kind of ministers they have for their worship.

CHAPTER THREE

Concerning the Ministers of Idolatry

THOSE WHOM we commonly call sorcerers, although it is rare for them to kill anyone by their witchcraft, are generally called *umu, laicca,* and, in some places, *chacha, auqui,* or *auquilla,* which means father or old man. But as they have various offices and ministries, so too they have their private names.

Huacapvíllac, meaning the one who talks to the huaca, is the most important. To him is entrusted the care of the huaca, the right to talk to it and to fabricate its replies to the town (although sometimes the Devil speaks to them through the stone).[1] It is his duty to bring offerings and make sacrifices,

---

[1] That is to say that the Devil really talks to them through the huaca.

to fast and have chicha made for the festival of the huacas. He must teach their idolatry, relate their fables, and reprove those who are careless about the worship and veneration of the huacas.

Malquipvíllac. It is his task to talk to the malquis, since his office is the same with regard to the malquis as that of the former with respect to the huacas.

Libiacpavíllac is of the same sort. He speaks to the lightning just as *punchaupvíllac* talks to the sun.[2]

Each of these men has his lesser minister or helper called *yanápac*.[3] And in many places, misapplying our word, they call him a sacristan because he serves in the sacrifices, for when the principal minister is absent he may take his place, though he does not always do so.

Macsa or *víllac*[a] are those who effect cures with their thousand tricks and superstitions. They make a sacrifice to the huacas or conopas of the persons who consult them. In the provinces we have visited, these persons have been found to be the most harmful because they are consulted for everything and asked to speak to the huacas, even though they do not have them in their keeping.[4]

Aucachic, called *ichuris*[5] in Cuzco, is the confessor. The office is never held by itself but is attached to that of víllac or macsa, just mentioned. This minister confesses everyone in his clan, including his own wife and children. The confessions take place during the festivals of the huacas or when the Indians are going on a long journey. The confessors are very scrupulous about their office, and I have met boys who had

[2] These are the priests of the sun and of the lightning and thunder.

[3] *Yanápac* was the minister's helper; *yana* is an employee of an inferior occupation; in domestic service they call them *yanacuna,* lowly people. See, concerning these Indians, the curious remarks of Cabello Balboa, *Historia del Perú,* Chap. IX, p. 120.

[4] Molina calls these *camasca.* Colección Urteaga, I, 21.

[5] According to Molina, Colección Urteaga, I, 23; Cobo, *Historia del Nuevo Mundo,* Vol. IV, Chap. XXXIII; Acosta, *Historia,* Bk. V, Chap. XXV.

[a] Spelled *viha* in the Spanish version. From internal evidence it is obvious that *víllac,* which appears below, is the correct form.

never confessed to a priest of the Lord Our God but who had confessed three or four times to these ministers of the Devil, as we shall see.

Açuac or *accac*[6] is one whose duty it is to make chicha for the festivals and offerings of the huacas. In the lowlands this is done by men, in the sierra by women, and in some places they choose girls for this task.

Sócyac is a way of casting lots or divination with corn. They make little piles of kernels without counting them, then they pick one up first from one pile and then from the other, and as they come out with an odd or an even number the luck is supposed to be good or bad.[7] In one town, the holder of this office showed us a bagful of little stones called *chunpirun*, which he said he had inherited from his grandfather for this purpose.

Rápiac is also a diviner and answers those who consult him by moving the fleshy parts of his arms. If he moves them to the right all will be well, if to the left the omen is bad.

Pacharícuc, pacchacatic, or *pachacuc,*[8] is a means of divination by the feet of the common hairy spider, which they call

[6] *Asua* or *acca* means *chicha.* See Tschudi, Colección Urteaga, IX, 39 ff. Dr. Angel Maldonado, "La Chicha," *Anales de la facultad de medicina,* 2nd Year, No. 2.

[7] "They call these doctors *camasca* or *soncoyoc.* When asked who gave them or taught them the profession they exercised they frequently replied that they had dreamed it, etc., etc." Cobo, *Historia del Nuevo Mundo,* Vol. IV, Bk. III, Chap. XXXV. *Camasca* is surely derived from the word *caman,* meaning talent, skill, cleverness, penetration, and, by extension, divining, foresight, knowledge of the future or of a secret. *Sancoyoc* is probably a foreshortening of *soncocamayoc,* the keeper of the heart, a name given to a doctor, since primitive man—and the common people even today—supposes life to be centered in the heart, and the evidence of existence in the beating of this organ, which they also regard as the center of love and of noble enthusiam. While annotating the *Información acerca de la religión de los incas* of Ondegardo, I formerly gave another interpretation of the word *soncoyoc.* This I now rectify because I believe the equivalence is ill founded. Ondegardo calls them sorcerers, but they were those who dedicated themselvs to the profession of curing. Colección Urteaga, III, Chap. X.

[8] *Pacharícuc, pachacutic,* or *pachacuc* is equivalent to divining by the use of spiders. It must be a foreshortening of *pacha aqui pachacutic. Pachca* means spider.

paccha and, sometimes, *oroso*. When they wish to consult them, they look in holes in the wall or beneath stones for spiders of this well-known species. They place them on a blanket or on the ground and chase them with a little stick until they break their legs. Then, looking to see which leg is missing, they perform divinations.

Móscoc[9] is divination through dreams. A person comes and asks whether he will get well or die of an illness, or whether he will find a lost horse, etc. The sorcerer who is consulted asks the Indian to give him his slingshot,[10] which he wears tied around his head, or for his *chuspa* or cloak, or some other article of clothing. If the inquirer is a woman, he asks for her *chumbi*, or sash, or something similar. These he takes home and sleeps on, then answers according to his dreams. If they consult him about love, he asks for a lock of hair or an article of clothing of the person he is divining about.

Hacarícuc, or *cuyrícuc*, is divination by the use of guinea pigs. The sorcerer cuts them open with his fingernail and divines by seeing where the blood comes out or which entrails move, a method often used by the pagan Romans.

All these offices and ministries are open to both men and women, including the confession, and there are some women who are renowned confessors, but commonly the principal offices are performed by men. An Indian I know, who was cook and butler for a priest, was also the confessor of the town. The Indians say:

"So-and-so is a good confessor. He gives light penance," or "so-and-so is not so good. He gives heavy penance."

Less important offices, such as that of diviner or chicha maker, are exercised by women. One can also include the *parianas* among the ministers, although they have not been punished nor counted among those listed in the towns. These are officers

---

[9] *Muscuc* means dreamer, derived from *muscuy*, dream.

[10] The *huaraca* is a slingshot. The Indians had the habit of wrapping the *huaraca* around their waists or around their heads. A striking example of the warrior with a *huaraca* wrapped around his head may be seen in the Natural History Museum of Lima. Concerning the slingshot, see H. H. Urteaga, *Armas en el antiguo Perú* (Lima, 1919).

chosen each year to guard the fields. They wear fox skins on their heads and carry staffs decorated with woolen tassels. They have to fast as long as their office lasts, or about two months, more or less, eating neither salt nor pepper, nor sleeping with their wives, and they change their voices, speaking in an affected and effeminate manner. Concerning all these matters and their origin, they tell many fables and traditions of their ancestors, and herein lies much superstition.

The office of priest of the huacas is achieved in one of three ways. The first is by succession, as when a son inherits it from his father. In case the heir does not have the use of his reason, his closest relative is chosen in his stead, and so on, until a legitimate heir, fit for the office, is found. The second way is by election. When the way of inheritance fails, or whenever they so decide, the other ministers elect someone who in the opinion of the curacas and caciques is most fitted for the task. For instance, a person who has been struck by lightning and has lived through it, even though he may have been crippled, is considered to be divinely chosen for the ministry of the huacas. The third way is for a person simply to assume the office on his own. Minor offices, such as divining and healing, are frequently entered upon in this manner. Old men and women often assume these functions in order to get enough to eat, entering the ministry by *vicçaraycu*, as they say, or *ventris causa*.

In a town in the province of Conchucos, visited by Licentiate Juan Delgado, there was a girl about fourteen years of age, of rare beauty. For this reason her parents and the caciques dedicated her to the service of a stone huaca named Chanca, which had the face of a person. They married her to this huaca, and everyone in town celebrated her wedding, staying out on a hill for three days with much carousing. They offered their sacrifices by the hand of this girl and considered it a proper and a lucky thing to do. They thought that sacrifices thus performed would be most acceptable to the huacas. The girl preserved her virginity as the other ministers had commanded her to do, for by marrying her to the huaca they had invested her with the sacred office of priestess. She was held in the greatest reverence and regarded as a divine and superior being. But when she heard the first sermon preached by the visitor she came forward and denounced herself, asking to be taught the principles of our faith and to be pardoned for her guilt.

A person about to assume one of the offices has to fast for a month, or, in some places, six, in others a year, eating neither salt nor pepper nor sleeping with his wife, nor washing nor combing his hair. In some localities they are forbidden to touch the body with their hands, and it is told of a man in San Juan de Cochas that during his time of fasting he neither washed nor combed his hair, and as a result his hair became infested with lice; in order to keep his oath and refrain from touching himself, he used a little stick to scratch with.

When the most important ministers see an Indian man or woman stricken by a sudden illness, deprived thereby of his reason, and acting insane, they say that the accident has happened because the huacas want him to be their víllac and priest. As soon as he comes to his senses they make him fast and study his office, for they believe that while they are talking to the huacas they must be deprived of their reason, either by the work of the Devil, who renders them foolish, or through chicha, which they drink whenever they intend to speak to a huaca. In Huacho one such minister was seized by a frenzy and ran around the fields like a madman. Eight or ten days later his relatives found him out on a hill, still beside himself. He was brought back to town and made a macsa and huacapvíllac. Similarly, everyone who suffers from heart disease is thought to have been chosen for the ministry.

In addition to the sorcerers already mentioned, the *cauchos*[11]

[11] *Caucho* is the appellation in the *chinchasuyo*[b] [*sic*] of the clever, intelligent, and diligent man. *Runa* is man, *p* is the genitive particle corresponding to *of* or *of the; micuy* is meal, or to eat.

[b] The Inca empire had four geographical divisions, one of which is *chinchasuyu*, or north. The others are: *collasuyu*, south; *intisuyu*, east; *contisuyu*, west. *Cuzco* meant navel or center, and the divisions were calculated from there.

of the towns of the lowlands and coast most properly deserve
the name. It took much effort and considerable trouble to find
them out because of the secrecy they maintain among themselves, and because the Indians are terrified of them. During
Dr. Avila's visit, the first to be found out was the sacristan
of the town, who was denounced by a Negro. These cauchos,
or *runapmícuc,* as they are called, are a kind of witch, which
is what the words mean. They have killed many people,
especially children. Some few traces and indications of them
had been found in towns previously visited, but it had not
been possible to find out what their evil office consisted of.
Finally, one day I was present while Dr. Hernando de Avendaño was conducting an examination in a certain town. There
was an Indian there, of good build, about twenty-five years
old, who had a cooperative attitude and a seemingly good
understanding of the usual ways of idolatry. He was being
sent away in peace because he had answered all the questions
that were put to him. But he said:

"Wait, sir, I have something to add. I really want to bare
my whole heart and become a good Christian."

After encouraging him to say whatever he wished and not
to be afraid, he told us that he was a witch, as his father had
been before him (and we afterward learned that the father
had been famous and much dreaded), and that he had learned
his office from him. He named many practicing witches.
Each of them was brought in and interrogated, first alone and
then confronted by the others, and extraordinary and horrible
deeds were found out. To sum up, in the various clans and
factions there are teachers of witchcraft whom they now
designate by our Spanish word for captain, and each of these
has his disciples and soldiers.

The captain warns his men at his discretion that they are
to come together on a certain night (for their meetings are
always held at night) and in a certain place. That night the
master goes to a house of his choice, accompanied by one or
two disciples. While they stand outside at the door he goes in,
scattering a powder made for the purpose from the bones of

the dead. Then using I know not what words and signs that he has prepared, he puts the entire household to sleep, so that no one in the house will move or hear anything. Then he goes up to the person he wants to kill, and with his fingernail takes blood out of some part of the body and sucks as much of it as he can. This is why in their language witches are called bloodsuckers. Then what they have sucked out in this manner they put into the palm of their hand or into a gourd and take it to where the rest are gathered. They say the Devil multiplies this blood or converts it into meat (I am inclined to believe that they add other meat to it) and they cook it together and eat it. The result is that the person whose blood has been sucked will die within two or three days. About eight or ten days before we arrived, a boy about sixteen years old had died, and as he lay dying he covered his face and said that he could see So-and-so, naming some of the witches who had come to kill him.

In these gatherings they have a common phraseology and way of speaking. They say: "Tonight we are going to eat the soul of so-and-so." I asked one of them what sort of meat it was and what it tasted like, and making signs of nausea he said that it was very bad and unpleasant and tasted like dried beef. The Devil appears to them in these assemblies, sometimes looking like a lion and sometimes like a tiger, sitting down and leaning on his elbows; they worship him devoutly.

The three qualities generally found in the witches are cruelty, idolatry, and depravity. A great deal has been learned about the first two, but little is known about the third. One of them remarked without shame or fear: "I have killed three boys," and another said, "I have eaten this many." When the visitor confronted them with each other in order to find out I know not what fact, one of them said: "You ate my son." "That is true," he answered, "I have already said so to the visitor. I ate him because you took away my farm." It is certain that when they are angry at each other they avenge themselves by eating each other's children, killing them as described, and they call this eating each other.

The priest of one town has said that a few years ago more than seventy children between the ages of twelve and eighteen died within four months, among them four sons of one woman within a single week. And now that the evil has been discovered it is suspected that they were all killed, for it was not known what disease they died of. During the visit, a witch died after making an earnest confession, but he sent for the visitor before his confession and told him he had been a witch for many years. He said that no one had taught him his witchcraft, but that he, I know not how, had obtained powders with which he put people to sleep. To find out whether they worked, he went one night to a town about a league and a half away from his own. He entered the first house that he wanted to, killed a boy, and returned home. Then, in order to make another test, he did it again. And so without any other reason he killed still another boy. One of their number told me with great feeling that he had been a witch against his will since the time he had been invited to go fishing by a neighbor who was a witch without his knowing it. The latter took him that night to a meeting where they forced him to eat. Then they said to him: "You are a witch. You must come whenever we call you. If you do not or if you denounce us we will kill you." Being afraid, therefore, he had continued to go to their diabolical meetings. Because these people are so dreaded, another Indian told me that once when he was in Lima a witch came in one night to kill him, and as he was awake he said to him:

"If you must kill me, don't do it here but in my own country where my relatives can bury me."

He never dared to mention this later to anyone or to denounce the witch. In four towns in the lowlands, sixty-three persons were found guilty of witchcraft; some were guilty, others less so. It is common knowledge that there are many more witches to be found in the towns of the coast, but none have been discovered in the towns in the sierra. After the visit, Dr. Alonso Osorio discovered a few in the mission of Cochamarca and thirty in the province of Ambar; and extraordinary and remarkable things like those that happened in the low-lands and on the coast were discovered.

All the abovementioned were sentenced in the place where they were discovered, but with a light sentence; this was mainly for the purpose of keeping them in custody while their just punishment was being decided, for to investigate all their murders and related crimes and to punish them properly would require an arm other than the ecclesiastical. Let us now examine their sacrifices.

CHAPTER FOUR

What Is Offered in Their Sacrifices and in What Manner

THE PRINCIPAL offering, the best and most important part of Indian sacrifices, is chicha. By it and with it the festivals of the huacas begin. It is everything. For its use they have receptacles and tumblers of many forms and materials. It is a common saying with them that when they go to worship the huacas they are giving them a drink. For each festival there are special ministers, as we have noted.[1] In the lowlands, from Chancay south, the chicha offered to the huacas is called *yale,* and it is made of *zora*[a] mixed with chewed corn. They also add powdered *espingo,*[b] and make it strong and thick. After they have poured it over the huaca to the extent they deem proper, the sorcerers drink the rest and it makes them act as if mad.

---

[1] We already have an excellent monograph on corn and chicha from the learned pen of those two intelligent and indefatigable scholars, Dr. Manuel Velásquez and Dr. Angel Maldonado. See *Anales de la facultad de medicina,* 2nd Year, Nos. 10 and 11.

[a] *Zora, sora,* or *jora,* a kind of corn much used in the making of chicha.

[b] The word first appears here but is not footnoted in the Spanish text until p. 46, n. 1. *Infra,* p. 44, n. 4.

In the sierra, chicha is sometimes made of a corn grown especially for the huaca, and that field is the first to be cultivated. No Indian may sow his own field ahead of this one. At other times they make chicha out of the first ripe ears of corn. The parianas, previously mentioned, pick them for this purpose. They make it strong and thick, like *mazamora*,^c which they call *tecti*. The women and girls chew the corn for this, and while so doing they must fast from salt and pepper and, if married, must abstain from relations with their husbands.

The llama, which we call the sheep of the land, is also sacrificed during the most solemn festivals of the huacas. They bring out an animal garlanded with flowers, tie him to a great stone,[2] and make him turn around five or six times. Then they cut open his left side, take out the heart, and eat it raw by the mouthful. They sprinkle the huaca with the blood and divide the meat among the ministers, giving some also to the rest of the Indians. In some places they raise young llamas especially for the huacas. In most of the towns of the sierra that have been visited, llamas have been purchased with silver, and the Indians have contributed to their purchase. At other times, Indians who own herds donate sheep and llamas to be sacrificed for the increase of the herd.

The most usual sacrifice is of guinea pigs, which they abuse not only for sacrifices but for divinations and healings with a multitude of tricks. If the Indians could be deprived of them

[2] The great stone where they tied the victims for the sacrifice was called *huatana*, or the place where the animal is tied. In Cuzco, under the cult of the sun, the *huatana* took the name of *intiphuatana*, the stone where the victim of the sun is tied. It has erroneously been believed that such stones, very common in the vast necropolis of ancient Peru, were sundials, the word *intiphuatana* being translated as measure of the sun or measure of the year, since *inti* is sun and *huata* is year. Such derivations have been discredited, and I think I have given conclusive reasons in my article addressed to the Sociedad geográfica de Lima concerning "Observatorios astronómicos de los incas." *Boletín de la Sociedad geográfica de Lima*, XXIX, Third Quarter, 40 ff. See also my study on the *intiphuatanas* in *El Perú—bocetos históricos*, Vol. I.

^c A dark red juice made from dark corn, much enjoyed in Peru to this very day. The liquid is drunk both fermented and unfermented.

it would be a good thing, but they all raise them in their homes and they multiply rapidly. They even have them in Rome. I was surprised to see them sold publicly here, so I asked, pretending innocence, what those little animals were, and they told me they were guinea pigs. As with everything else, they have their huacas and conopas to make them multiply. While I was writing about guinea pigs an Indian brought me a small one carved in stone, which was his conopa. To sacrifice them they usually cut them open in the middle with their thumbnail. I once saw this done by two Indians who were being examined by Dr. Avila. They also drown them in a gourd of water, holding the head down until the animal dies, talking all the while to the huaca. Then they cut them open from top to bottom with ridiculous ceremonies, this is the usual way to kill them for use in divining.

In some places silver is offered up in the form of reales. In Libia Cancharco fifteen silver duros[d] were found, together with some small pieces of ordinary silver. In the town of Recuay, Dr. Ramírez found two hundred duros in a huaca. They generally hammer the coins or chew them in such a way that you can hardly see the royal arms. Coins are also found around huacas, looking as if stained with blood or chicha. On other occasions, the priests of the huacas keep the silver that is collected as offerings to be spent for their festivals.

Coca is a very common offering, whether raised for the purpose or purchased. The most carefully selected coca fields are those belonging to the huaca, and the community tills and cultivates them. About two leagues from the town of Cajamarquilla, on the bank of the river Huamanmayu, which is the same as Barranca (because coca grows only in very hot country), there were fourteen small coca fields belonging to huacas of towns in the sierra. Indians are set to guard these fields, to gather the coca, and take it to the ministers of the huaca at the proper time, for it is a universal offering for huacas on all occasions. These fields we ordered to be burned.

Bira, which is a name for llama fat, is also an offering which

[d] Large Spanish coin about the size of a silver dollar.

they burn in front of the huacas and conopas. There is also a superstitious trick that they sometimes play. In Parquín, before the visitor Hernando de Avendaño went there, they made a sacrifice to burn his soul, as they put it. They make a small lump or figurine out of fat and then burn it. They say they do this in order to burn the soul of the judge or other person whose soul they want to destroy. Their phrase for it is that he will become mad or lose his reason and sensibility. This is done in a particular way, for if the soul they are to burn is Spanish, the figurine to be burned must be made out of pork fat. Viracocha,[e] they say, does not eat llama fat. But if an Indian's soul is to be burned, they use a different fat, mixed with corn flour. When the soul is Spanish they use wheat flour. This trick, or sacrifice, is used on many occasions, and they use it against people they are afraid of, such as *corregidors,* visitors, and the like. The rite is called *caruay-quispina,*[3] and it is performed even today where these persons are expected to pass to keep them from reaching the town, and so forth.

They offer up whole corn sometimes and at other times corn meal, which they burn with coca and fat. Espingo is a small dry fruit, round like an almond, and of a very bright color,[4] though not very good to taste. They bring it from Chachapoyas and say it is medicinal for pains in the stomach, hemorrhages, and other illnesses. They take it in powdered form and pay a high price for it. It used to be sold for this purpose, and many years ago, in Jaen de Bracamoros, the Indians paid their tribute in espingo. The previous Lord Archbishop, knowing it to be a common offering for the huacas, prohibited its sale to the Indians under penalty of excommunication. In the lowlands among the Indians that

[3] *Carua,* a word unknown to the glossaries, is perhaps equivalent to a human figure or doll. *Qquespina* is equivalent to guard, remedy, or defense, and, by extension, refuge. Perhaps with this sacrifice they warded off or defended themselves against the harm they expected to receive from the persons who were the object of the charm.

[4] *Espingo.* Tree indigenous to Peru. See Cobo, *Historia del Nuevo Mundo,* Vol. II, Bk. IV, Chap. XC, p. 95.

[e] God of the source of life.

have been visited, there is not one who does not have some espingo in his possession if he owns a conopa.

Aut is another small dry fruit, not very different from espingo. This too is brought from around Chachapoyas and is said to be medicinal also.

Astop tuctu are red plumes, or those of other colors, from the *huacamaya* birds or other birds of the Andes which they call *asto; tuctu* means plume, or something that sprouts.

Huachua are the white plumes of a bird of the same name to be found in the lagoons and on the *puna.*[f]

Pariuna are the pink plumes of a similar bird, of that name.[5]

Mullu is a large sea shell that they all have pieces of.[6] An Indian gave me a piece, smaller than a fingernail, that he had bought for four reales. The Indians on the coast, and even the Spaniards, make a profit out of selling these shells to the Indians of the sierra. Yet they hardly know why they buy them. On occasion they make beads of mullu and place them with their huacas. They also have other uses for these beads in their confessions, as we shall see later.

Paria[7] are powders of a vermilion color, brought from the mines of Huancavelica and made from the metal from which mercury is derived, though its appearance is more like that of lead oxide.

Binços are fine blue powders. *Llacsa* is a green color in the form of either powder or stone, like copper oxide.

[5] *Pariana*, or *parihuana*, is a bird of red and white plumage common to Lake Titicaca, Chinchaycocha, and Parinacochas, which last name is perhaps a foreshortening of Parianacocha, or lagoon of the parianas. "*Pariana*, the rosy plumes of the flamingo (Phoenicopteras ignipallaitus and Ph. Andinas, Philip), an offering also much sought after for sacrifices. This pink crane is also called *Pariana*." Tschudi, *Civilización y lingüística de Perú antiguo*, Colección Urteaga, X, 231. Ondegardo, Colección Urteaga, III, 39.

[6] *Mullu, mollo-mollo.* "They sacrificed sea shells which they call *mullu*, red and yellow and shaped like corn." Molina, Colección Urteaga, I, 28, 80, and 102. Ondegardo, Colección Urteaga, III, 39. "This shaped *mollo*, which is also called *chaquira*, is altogether harmful, since it is used for all sorts of sacrifices and rites," says Licentiate Polo.

[7] *Paria* is mercury sulphide, taken from the mercury mines of Huancavelica and much prized as an offering. Tschudi, Colección Urteaga, X, 231.

[f] The high, cold plains of the Andes.

Carvamuqui are yellow powders.

Parpa, or *sancu,* is a ball of corn meal kept for sacrifices.[8]

Among other things that are offered up are their eyelashes, which they pull out and blow toward the huaca as an offering.

All the abovementioned powders of different colors are offered by blowing them, as they do their eyelashes, and they point to the conopas and huacas to attract their attention before they blow. In the province of Yauyos they do the same thing with silver in a ceremony they call *huatcuna.* The rest of their offerings, which are made in small quantities, they have the ministers burn, but only on the occasions of which we shall now speak.

CHAPTER FIVE

The Festivals Celebrated for the Huacas

AFTER THE visits had begun, in the towns where they were expected the Indians stopped celebrating the festivals of the huacas with as much solemnity as before. Individuals have said during confession that they put aside their huacas when they heard that a visitor was on his way. But where the visits have not yet begun and are not expected, they carry on their festivals up to this very day. Not more than a week ago an individual reported that he found himself in the midst of one, and that in a town not far from here the Indians celebrated a festival, though not one of the most important ones, not more than two months ago. The most important festivals are celebrated with a tremendous show of happiness and joy, for tradition says they were begun by the very huacas for whom they are celebrated. The first thing that is done at festival time is by the chief sorcerer who is

---

[8] A mass of corn meal, mixed with salt. See Villagómez, *Introducción contra las ceremonias y ritos de los indios,* Colección Urteaga, XII, 207, n. 2.

in charge of the huaca, who tells the caciques and other Indians to prepare the chicha they will drink. While this is being done, the priest asks everyone for offerings of mullu, paria, *llacsa*, guinea pigs, and the like, as we have seen. When these are collected, the sorcerer goes on the appointed day with his helpers or sacristans to the principal huaca. Sitting down on the ground and stretching out his left hand toward it, he says:

"Señor X [naming the huaca, and making the usual sound with his lips as if sucking them in, which they call *mochar*], Here I come bringing the things your children and creatures offer you. Accept them and do not be angry. Give them life, health, and good fields."

Saying this and similar things, he pours out the chicha in front of the huaca, or over it, or sprinkles the huaca with it as if he were giving it a rap on the nose. He anoints the huaca with the blood of guinea pigs or llamas and then burns, or blows toward it, the rest of the offerings, according to the nature of each one.

In like manner he approaches the lesser huacas and malquis. When he returns after these sacrifices, the Indians stay awake all night, singing, dancing, or telling stories. Even the children are punished if they fall asleep. They call this *pacarícuc*,[a] and on this night their fast begins. They eat neither salt nor pepper nor sleep with their wives. This festival usually lasts five days, in some places longer, according to various traditions.

During the fast the Indians all make confession to their confessor. The listener and the one who is confessing sit down on the ground in a place in the fields chosen for the purpose. They do not confess inward sins but such sins as having stolen or mistreated someone or having had more than one wife (though they do not deem it a sin to have concubines). They also accuse themselves of adulteries, but mere fornication is not regarded as sinful. They blame themselves for not having appealed to the huacas, and the sorcerer tells them to mend their ways, etc. The Indian then places the powders for the

[a] Not to be confused with pacharícuc. *Supra*, pp. 34-35.

offering on a flat stone and blows them. The confessor holds a little stone called *pasca*, meaning pardon, which is brought to him by the Indian. The confessor rubs the Indian's head with the stone and washes him with corn meal and water in a stream where two rivers meet. And this is called *tincuna*. They think it very sinful to withhold sins when confessing, and the confessor takes great pains to find everything out. There are various ceremonies for this purpose, depending on the locality. In some places, when the Indian comes to the confessor, he says: "Hear me ye hills round about, and ye plains and flying condors, and the eagle owl and the barn owl, for I wish to confess my sins." He says all this holding in two fingers of his right hand a bead made of mullu, or sea shell, fixed upon a thorn. He raises up the thorn as he tells his sins and concludes by giving it to his confessor. The latter takes it and presses the thorn into a blanket until the bead breaks. Then he looks to see how many pieces there are. If it has broken into three the confession has been a good one; if two, the confession has not been good and he tells him to confess his sins again.

In other places a confession is verified by picking up a handful of *ichu*,[b] and from this the word *ichuri* has been derived, which means one who gathers straw. The confessor divides the straw into two piles. Then he picks up a straw first from one side and then from the other until he can see whether the piles are even. If even the confession is good, if uneven bad. In still other places they practice divining with the blood of guinea pigs. In a town near here the penitent's hands are tied behind him when the confession is over, and the confessor tightens the cord until he tells the truth. An Indian told the visitor today in my presence that his confessor had struck him with a stick to force him to confess all his sins. Another said that he had been beaten with a rope. For penance they are assigned the usual fasting: not to eat salt nor pepper and to refrain from sleeping with their wives. One said that he had been told to fast in this manner for six months.

[b] A coarse grass that grows on the high plateau or puna.

They confess to the sorcerers not only at festival time but when they are ill, and they believe that their illness has come because their malquis and huacas are angry at them.

There is still another way for the Indians to purify themselves of their sins without telling them to anyone else, and that is to rub their heads with their pasca and wash their heads in the river. They say that in this way the water takes away their sins.

An Indian in a lowland town told me that a sorcerer had led him and his wife to an irrigation ditch and washed them there and made them put on new clothes; he told them to leave the clothes they had worn on the way, saying that their sins had been left behind, and that whoever put on their clothes would carry them all away with him.

Confessions are made during the solemn festivals, of which there are three each year. The most important of these is close to Corpus Christi, or even at the same time. It is called Oncoy[1] Mitta, which is when the constellation called Oncoy[c] appears. They do homage to this constellation to keep their corn from drying up. The other important festival is at the beginning of the rainy season, at Christmas or a little afterward. This festival is addressed to the thunder and lightning, to beg for rain.[2] The third is when they harvest the corn, which they call ayrihuamita, because they do the dance of ayrihua[3] at that time. On all these occasions there are fastings and confessions; when these are over, they drink and dance

[1] *Oncay, Ancay, Cuzqui* for Ondegardo. See Colección Urteaga, III, 21, also p. 26, concerning the dances of the festival of Oncoy; these dances are called *llama* or *huacón* dances. See Molina, Colección Urteaga, I, 32, and nn. 85 and 86.

[2] They call the month of December *Camay Quilla*. See Molina, Colección Urteaga, I, 78. "In the morning those who had them in charge brought out the huacas of the Maker, Sun, Thunder, Moon, etc." *Ibid.*, 80.

[3] *Ayrihua*, the dance which was performed during the fiesta of the gathering of the corn in May. Concerning the dance and the festival of ayrihuaymita, see Molina, Colección Urteaga, I, 24. Ondegardo, Colección Urteaga, III, 21, n. 34. Tschudi, Colección Urteaga, X, Appendix, 225. See also *supra*, pp. 30-31, n. 21.

[c] The Seven Goats, or Pleiades. *Supra*, p. 23, n. *a*.

and sing. The women play little drums, which they all have, and some sing and others respond, and the men play instruments called *succhas*,[d] made from deers' heads, which they call guaucu,[e] and of these instruments and horns they have a great supply. All this is burned on the day of the exhibitions.

While they are singing these songs, which tell foolish things about their ancestors, they invoke the huaca by name, raising their voices and reciting a single verse, or they raise their hands or turn around, according to the custom of the region. They do not generally pronounce the name of the huaca all at once, but by syllables, interpolating sounds between the syllables without articulating any one syllable clearly. For these performances they wear their best clothes, made of cumbi, and on their heads they wear something like half-moons of silver, called *chacrahinca*, or other objects called huama, and little round medals called *tincurpa*, or clasps. Their shirts have ornaments of dangling silver balls, slingshots with silver buttons, huacamaya plumes of various colors, and a kind of ruff made of feathers sometimes called a huaca and, in other places a *tamta*. All these ornaments they keep for such occasions.

When the festival is over, in some places they sacrifice guinea pigs in order to find out by the way the blood runs in the entrails, or some other part of the animal, whether they have fasted well and kept all the ceremonies of the festival. This rite is *callpacta ricusum*.

When they address the huaca they call it *runapcámac*, or creator of man, and such names which should be given to God only. They ask the huaca for life and health and food to eat, etc. They never ask for anything concerning the other life. The same pleas are made to their malquis. It is to be

[d] The Incas had drums of all sizes and shapes. The *succhas* were skulls of the guanaco, as Father Arriaga tells us. The best treatise on Inca music is by all odds that of Stevenson, *The Music of Peru*. In this particular instance he is not too enlightening, however, since he takes his definition of the *succha* from this work.

[e] *Sic* for guanaco, a cameloid smaller than the llama. Its hair is finer, and it is less readily tamed.

noted that not all the Indians see the principal huaca, nor enter the place or house where it is, but only the sorcerers, who talk to it and bring it offerings. In the town of Xampai, in the mission of Gorgor, a sorceress told the Indians that they must cover their eyes to worship the huaca Xampai, because the divine essence could not be perceived by human eyes. They told this to Dr. Osorio. For the Devil has put them in such fear of their huacas that even the very sorcerers, when they go with the crown agent to bring the huacas to the visitor, simply point to them when they are two or three steps away. Finally, however much they resist, they are made to approach them without fear. In the town of Cochas an Indian was sent to fetch a huaca, and before crossing the bridge over the river Barranca he rubbed the huaca well with garlic. On being asked why he had done so, he said that this was so it would not knock the bridge down. When we ask an Indian whether he has worshiped or adored huacas, this does not mean whether he has seen them or gotten down on his knees before them, because worship does not consist in this, but in coming together for festivals in places chosen for the purpose near the huaca. When they have made the offerings brought by the priest they invoke the huaca, as we have said, by raising their left hand and opening it toward the huaca with a motion as if they were kissing it. On such occasions they must wear no Spanish clothing, nor any hat or shoes. Even the caciques, who are generally dressed like Spaniards, wear traditional clothes on these occasions.

They worship the sun and the lightning in this same fashion, and when they come down from the sierra to the lowlands, they look upon the sea and worship it also. They pull out their eyelashes and offer them, and they beg to stay well and return in health and with much silver to their own country, as we have noted, for the seed time at mamapacha. Outside of festive occasions, it is common for them to beg or invite or hire a sorcerer to come and present their offerings to the huacas and confess them when they are ill. An Indian of the lowlands told me that the sorcerer of a certain huaca led him out for some distance, and after drinking a great deal he took him on his shoulders and said, addressing the huaca by name:

"Señor So-and-so, here is your son coming to give you something to drink, and to ask you for health, and so forth."

In the town of Huacho, when they went to the islands for guano, near the headlands of Huaura, they poured out chicha as a sacrifice on the beach to keep the balsa boats from capsizing. Before this, there were two days of fasting. When they reached the island they worshiped a huaca named Huaman-cántac as lord of the guano and made offerings to him so that he would let them take the guano. On their return to the mainland, they fasted two more days and then danced, sang, and drank. And except for these festive occasions, or during sickness, at seed time, or when they are in trouble, they do not remember their huacas very much, nor even their conopas, or household gods. Nor do they worship them, except on the occasions we have mentioned.

CHAPTER SIX

The Abuses and Superstitions of the Indians

INDIAN superstitions and abuses are as different and diverse as are their provinces and towns, for as regards a single subject some have one superstition, others another. They only agree by being in error and mistaken in their beliefs. I shall demonstrate how in the matters already seen and touched, so to speak, some of the practices in villages not yet visited are either the same or similar to those in towns already visited.

When a woman is in childbirth, they send for the sorcerer to sacrifice to the conopa that the woman calls her own. He places it upon her breast or holds it over her so that the birth will be normal. On such occasions, in some places they invoke the moon, as the Romans did under the name of Lucina.

As we have already noted, when twins are born they call them chuchus or curi, and in Cuzco *taqui huahua,* and they believe that twins are a sacrilegious and abominable thing, although they say that one of them is the son of lightning. They do penance on this account as if they had committed a terrible sin. Usually the father and mother both fast for many days, as Dr. Avila has shown, eating neither salt nor pepper nor having intercourse at that time. In some places they carry this on for six months. In others, both father and mother lie down on one side and remain without moving for five days. One foot is folded under them, and a lima bean or kidney bean is placed under the knee, until with the effect of perspiration it begins to grow. For the next five days they do the same thing on the other side, all the while fasting as described. When this penance is over, the relatives go hunting for a deer, and after cutting it up they make a kind of canopy of the skin. The penitents pass beneath this with ropes around their necks, which they must wear for many days.

Last July, in the mission of Mangas, in the *corregidor* district of Cajatambo, an Indian woman gave birth to twins, and her penance was to remain on her knees for ten days with her hands on the ground, without changing position during this time for any reason. She became so thin and disfigured from this ordeal that the priest who found her in this situation did not dare to punish her, as it seemed dangerous to do so. In other places, there are like superstitions for such cases.

When a baby is born feet first, which they call chacpas, they have similar abuses, the worst of which is that if they succeed in hiding these children they do not have them baptized, and if either chacpas or chuchus die young, they are kept in the house in earthenware jars. Of these mummies we burned a great many in various towns.

The Indians are very superstitious about naming their children. The important ones bear the name of a huaca, and a festival is celebrated when the name is bestowed. They call this baptizing, or name-giving. There is also an abuse in this connection that is so commonplace that no one notices it, and it is this: every time thereafter that their name is called, they say the Indian name before the Christian or baptismal name. Thus they do not say "Pedro Paucar Líbiac," but "Paucar Líbiac Pedro." They also have superstitions concerning the name Santiago. They often give this name to one of the chuchus, as a son of lightning, which they call Santiago. I do not think this is because of the name Boanerges, which Christ Our Lord gave to the Apostle Saint James and his brother, Saint John, calling them lightning, or sons of thunder, according to the Hebrew phrase. It is probably because the phrase has been brought here or suggested by the young Spaniards who, when it thunders, say that Saint James's horse is running. Or perhaps they have noticed that when the Spaniards wage war, they shout before shooting their arquebus, which the Indians call *illapa*, or lightning, "Santiago! Santiago!" However this may be, they have taken over the name Santiago and attach superstition to it. For this reason, among other rules laid down by the visitors at the end of a visit is this one: that no Indian should be named Santiago, but Diego instead.

When the Indian children have grown somewhat, say to the age of four or five, they have their hair cut for the first time. This is done superstitiously, inviting all the relatives, especially the *massas* and *cacas*.[a] For the occasion they fast and celebrate a festival to the huaca to whom they offer the young child. To the child they give wool, corn, sheep, silver, and other things. On this occasion his name is changed as noted above, as is that of the father and mother, to that of the huaca or malquis. The hair that is cut off they call pacto or *huarca* in the general language, *ñaca* in the lowlands and pacto in the sierra, and in some places they make an offering of this hair or send it to the huaca or dangle it in front of it. In other places, the hair is kept in the house as a sacred object. We burned a quantity of this hair, or pacto, in the towns we visited.

When they put the *huarás*, or breechclouts, on their children

[a] Sons-in-law and maternal uncles.

at the age of eight or ten, practically the same superstitions are displayed. They say that they used to sacrifice to Lucifer, whom in this province they call Huárac, and perhaps the word Huarás is an allusion to this. Another common abuse among the Indians of today is to have carnal knowledge of each other several times before marriage, and it is rare for them not to do so. This custom is called *tincunacuspa,* and they are deeply rooted in this malpractice. In a town that I was passing through an Indian boy asked me to marry him to his betrothed. One of her brothers, however, objected strongly, giving no other reason except that they had never slept together. I also know another Indian who refused to see his wife after their marriage and treated her harshly. He alleged that she was a woman of low condition since no one had ever loved her or had carnal knowledge of her before marriage.

At death and in the burial of the dead they also have a great many abuses and superstitions. Under the winding shroud they frequently dress the dead in new clothing, whereas at other times they merely lay the folded clothing on top of them without actually putting it on. They perform the pacarícuc, or all-night vigil, with sad songs, sung either in chorus or as solos, with the rest of the people responding. Then, when the dead man is carried out, they close up the door that he passes through and never use it again.

In some localities they scatter corn meal or *quinua*[b] meal about the house in order to find out,[1] so they say, by the tracks in the meal whether the person has come back.

In some towns in the lowlands, the clan comes together with the relatives ten days after a death occurs to accompany the nearest relative to a spring or flowing stream that has been agreed upon. There they duck him three times and wash all the dead person's clothes. After this, they have a picnic at

[1] The custom of sprinkling flour on the floor of the room where the sick man died in order to tell by the traces or footsteps whether the dead return is still practiced in Indian towns in the present departments of Cajamarca and Amazonas. In most of the cases observed by the present writer, flour was replaced by well-scattered ashes.

[b] A nutritive Andean grain that grows at high altitudes.

which they spit out the first mouthful of food they chew. When their drunkenness is over, they return to the house and block off the dead person's room. They throw out the rubbish while the sorcerers sing, and they keep on singing and drinking all the next night for the soul of the dead. They say he returns to eat and drink, and when they are well into their wine they say the soul is coming, and they pour out a lot of wine[2] and offer it to him. The next morning they say the soul is now in Zamayhuaci, or the house of rest, and will never return again. The pacarícuc[3] usually lasts five days, during which they fast, eating only white corn and meat and abstaining from salt and pepper. And they play a game called *pisca* which uses the names of five days. It is played with little sticks with stripes. I do not believe there is any mysterious reason for this but that it is used to beguile their sleepiness. When the five days are up, they wash the dead man's clothes in the river.

They pour chicha discreetly into the tomb so that the dead may drink, and they make a show of doing him honor, placing cooked meals and roasts upon the grave for him to eat. For this reason, it has been forbidden them to place anything of this sort upon a grave on All Saints Day.

Their greatest abuse is to disinter the dead and remove their bodies to their machays, or burial places of their ancestors in the fields. In some localities they call these *zamay*, which means tomb of rest. At the time of death they cry out: "Zamarcam," that is, "*Requievit*."[4] On being asked why they do this, they say that this is cuyaspa, for the love they bear them. They say that the dead lying in the church are in great torment and bound to the earth, whereas in the fields, because they are in the open air and not buried, they have more rest. A few days before we reached a certain town, an influential Indian and his wife had taken the bodies of their two children away from the church. To accomplish their purpose they

[2] The wine to which Father Arriaga alludes was chicha (acca or azua), called the wine of the natives by some of the chroniclers.
[3] *Pacaric*, what is reborn, what returns, the dawn. *Pisca* is a variant of *pishga* or *pichca*, equivalent to five.
[4] *Zamay* means rest. *Requievit* is a Latin word meaning rest.

buried them one after the other in a sort of crypt made of stone slabs, and they carried them into their house and kept them there two days, celebrating a great festival, dressing them in new clothes, and carrying them around town in a procession. And they invited their relatives to drink at the festival. After that they returned to the church. We made them dig the bodies up again and, after destroying their crypt, we made them throw earth upon them. It is to be observed how important it is for us never to consent to their burying bodies in crypts.

They do not hold the same opinion as we do concerning persons who hang themselves. They think of them as more than human and invoke them and call upon them for certain things. Perhaps this is why in some places they hang themselves with so little hesitation. A few months ago there was a case of an influential Indian youth who was boasting in a festival of drunkenness to some Indian girls with whom he had an evil friendship. They thought he was joking when he said to them one night at the end of the fiesta:

"I want to find out which of you is fond of me and will come and hang herself with me."

Saying this, he left the house, and they looked for him everywhere, thinking that he had gone off somewhere. But they came upon him hanging near that very house. Furthermore, a little more than a month ago the visitor imprisoned a sorcerer and put manacles on him, but he did not press him nor force him particularly. Rather, he coaxed him and gave him things to eat from his own table during the two days that he was a prisoner in his own room. One night the man went out quietly without being heard, and taking the length of the thin cord they wear around their heads, called a *huaraca*, or slingshot, he hanged himself in the doorway by drawing up his knees. When I went out at daybreak I found him in this position, facing our room. We had him dragged out of town by the feet and burned his body in order to frighten the rest of them.

The *huacanquis*, or *manchucu*, as they call them in the lowlands, is the same as the love potion the Greeks and Romans speak of, which makes one person fall in love with another. This is in common use everywhere.[5] They are made out of the hair of the person by whom they wish to be loved, or out of multicolored birds brought from the Andes. Or they make them out of the plumes of these same birds, or out of brightly colored butterflies, mixed with other things.

It is common, especially among men who are in love, if they want to find out if a certain woman loves them, to throw a pebble at some large split rock or hollow stone and see if it lands in the crack or hollow. Sometimes, instead of throwing a stone, they toss small straight sticks which they call *huachi*, at the opening, until one of them finally lands. Then they tell the girl to come and see what fate has decided. There is great abuse and deceit in this, for the woman for whom this ceremony is performed never refuses. The ceremony is called *cacahuachi*, meaning a crag pierced by an arrow. If they succeed in putting the stick into the opening, it is sign that the person of whom they are making a trial loves them, whereas if they fail she does not. Those who have seen this superstition, or are acquainted with it, will realize that it is done without malice. The proof is called *sipastarina*, in order to sleep with a woman, as one might phrase it.

An even more harmful abuse than this one was discovered and punished by Dr. Osorio during his visit. During the month of December, when the avocados are beginning to ripen, they celebrate a festival called Acatay mita to aid the ripening process, and this lasts six days and six nights. The men and boys gather in a clearing in the orchards and run up a long hill, completely nude. If they catch a woman during the race, they possess her then and there. The festival is preceded by an all-night vigil and five days of fasting, during which they eat neither salt nor pepper nor have anything to do with women.

The women for their part had another abuse. When they

[5] Among the Chachapoyas Indians a mysterious amulet or philter to provoke love was called *piripiri* and was extracted from an odoriferous wood from the forests of the Amazon.

want to have children, they pick up small stones at random and wrap them up and swaddle them in woolen yarn. Then they make an offering of them by leaving them beside some large stone venerated for this purpose. Twelve leagues from Cajatambo we found many of these stones, wrapped up like children, under an overhanging rock. Some caciques whom we met there on the road told us about the superstition concerning these stones, and so we removed them. We also threw down the hill a stone thus wrapped which they call a *huassa*.

There used to be and there still is a very common custom that when the Indians are climbing a hill or grow tired on the road, they pick out a large stone on the path ahead, and when they reach it they spit coca or chewed corn on it (and for this reason they call the stone and the ceremony *tocanca*). On other occasions, they abandon their sandals, an old shoe, or their huaraca,[c] or some ropes, or little bundles of ichu or straw. Or they place little stones upon it and so in this way, they say, they get rid of their weariness. By verbal corruption, these heaps of stones are generally called *apachitas*, and some say they worship them. Yet they are nothing but stones which they have been piling up through superstition, offering them to any power that will take away their weariness and help them carry their load. For this is the apachita mentioned by Garcilaso el Inca, a native of Cuzco, in his *Annals of Peru*. He said he learned about it from the papers of Father Blas Valera, of our Society.

When they build their houses, as in everything else that they do, they practice many superstitions. They usually invite the members of their clan. They pour chicha on the cement as an offering and sacrifice to keep the house from falling down, and when it is finished they sprinkle it with chicha again. In the sierra, if they take a drink while they are building the house, no drop must fall, for if it does they say the house will leak and will have a lot of holes in it. And in certain localities they give the house the name of the idol to which it is dedicated.

[c] Slingshot. *Supra,* p. 35, n. 10.

In the sierra, when there is a mist, which occurs frequently and is very dense during rainy season, the women make a noise with the silver and copper clasps which they wear on their breast and blow on them, for they say this will clear away the mist and brighten the day. During the rainy season, to stop a downpour they burn salt or throw ashes into the wind.

The ancient customs that were followed during eclipses of the moon are called *quillamhuañun,* meaning "the moon dies," or *quilla tutayan,* "the moon grows dark." They still do this, whipping the dogs, beating drums, and shouting through the town to bring the moon back to life.

There are superstitions and abuses in other matters too (for there is hardly any aspect of life in which they do not have them), but because they have not been well authenticated, I shall refrain from mentioning them. All are branches and leaves growing out of the trunk of their paganism and idolatry. Experienced persons, therefore, believe that they maintain today the same ceremonies as they had before the coming of the Spaniards, but that they perform them secretly and that the Devil does not speak to them so frequently nor so publicly as before. Let us now examine the roots to which a remedy must be applied, instead of stopping, so to speak, at the branches.

CHAPTER SEVEN

Concerning the Roots and Causes of the Idolatry That Is Found among the Indians Today

THE CHIEF source and root of the evil so common in this archbishopric, which we fear is to be encountered throughout the kingdom, is the failure to teach Christian doctrine; if this could be remedied the remaining sources and roots would dry up and disappear. For even though we call every curacy among the Indians a *doctrina* or mission, in some places it is so in name only. In towns where a crown agent is stationed, or where the best trained of the boys can repeat the rudiments, or sing them, or teach them to the youngsters who come together every day, or tell them to the people of the town on Wednesdays and Fridays, Christian teaching is not assumed to be lacking. *But the fact is that even under such conditions* those who recite do so in a parrotlike manner without any understanding of what they are saying. When asked questions they reply in chorus, but if one of them is questioned by himself, not one in twenty knows the Christian doctrine, that is to say, the rudiments. *And if the boys are the most knowledgeable in this, how much less do the old men know.*[a] One of the greatest tasks yet to be accomplished in the missions is to teach the Indians and to examine each one separately. This is quite essential before confessing them. Once taught and examined, they are handed a token to give to their confessor when they go to confession. The confessor then gives them another so that they may be written down on the list of those who have confessed. It has also been necessary on reaching a town to see whether the crown agent or the boys who teach Christian doctrine really know it well, because in some localities they teach badly, changing and inverting some of the words or letters so that the sense is garbled. For instance, in the credo, instead of saying *hucllachacuininta*, meaning Communion, or gathering of the saints, they say *pucllachacuininta*, meaning the jest or merriment of the saints. Thus, even in the matter of Christian teaching, we have discovered that they are subject to mistakes and errors arising from the fact that many priests leave even this shadow and image of Christian teaching to the crown agent or to certain boys. They scorn to teach it themselves and pay little attention as to whether it is being taught well or ill. And if they do not perform this small task, how can we expect them to do what is most important, that is, to preach and teach the mysteries of the faith and lead the Indians out of their errors and deceits?

[a] Italics in the original.

Many priests carry out their duties exactly as they should, but even some who know the language have little or no familiarity with preaching in it. Others do not know the language and still less what to preach. They have no books nor do they want any. Others have a good tongue and skill in preaching but do not do so because, as they say, they have fallen *in communem errorem*. When they preach they do so for duty's sake, unwillingly, and without really trying to instruct.

There is still another obstacle that must be understood by those who can and should remedy it, and that is, that the Christian missions have several towns in their charge, and although there are priests zealous for the good of the Indians, they are unable to visit them according to their necessity. I could name towns that never see a priest except on All Saints Day, the day of the Church's Vocation, or some such occasion. In many towns, the Gospel has never been preached nor the mysteries of the faith, except for the mere rudiments. We can even regard a mission as good and its teacher a good one if a third of the Indians know that much. For although the councils, synods, and prelates of this archbishopric, especially His Illustrious Lordship (may he live many years) who now governs, have taken firm measures, including everything that has been suggested for a remedy, all these measures put together are as yet ineffective. As the Catalan proverb says, *si cor non mous, en vano te caramillo.*[b] Many priests because they are not moved by a heartfelt zeal for the good of the Indian soul not only do not teach their Indians but make fun of those who do. They say that to do so is an impertinence and that the Indians do not need to know theology. This I actually heard one of them say. This lack of Christian teaching is the whole mischief. *Hoc opus hic labor est.*

The total ignorance of the Indians in the matters of our faith stems from this lack of Christian instruction and teaching. And before God and man, the Indians are less to blame for

[b] "If your heart does not move you, in vain do I play the flute for you." Not a common or well-known proverb.

this than those who have failed to teach them. After all, one has an excuse for not knowing mathematics if he has never heard of the subject. So the Indians go on saying: "They have never taught me that. They have never said that to me."

No boy, however young he is, fails to know the name of his clan's huaca, and to put this to the test I have questioned many of them. Yet I cannot remember one who was unable to name his huaca. Few, however, when asked: who is God? or, who is Jesus Christ? can answer.

This ignorance is the cause of the errors they believe in so firmly and to which they are so strongly attached. They do not know that we all come from our first parents. They are persuaded that the Spaniards have one origin and the Negroes another and think also that each Indian faction and clan has its separate origin and pacarina. This they call by a private name and invoke, worship, and offer sacrifices to, calling it *camac*, which means creator. Each one says he has his own creator. Some say it is a hill, others a spring. Others tell fables and imaginings of their pacarinas like the stories of Huacho and Begueta: that the sun came down to earth and laid two eggs, one of gold, from which the curacas and caciques are descended, the other of silver, from which the rest of the Indians came. To the same end others tell long fables similar to those imagined by the poets of the *Deucalion* and *Pirrha*. These, because they are long and as numerous as the very towns and clans, I shall refrain from telling. I only wish to repeat what I have already said, that this is why the Indians are so pertinacious and stubborn in preserving their sites and ancient towns and in returning to them after they have been consolidated with other towns. They regard them as their fatherland and pacarina, and they say that although there are discomforts in these places and comforts in others, by this the saying *Dulcis amor patriae ratione valentior omni* is verified.

They have no fewer deceits and errors concerning their final end than they have about their origin, although they have fewer words to describe it and fewer dwelling places in the former than in the latter. A common error in all the towns that have been visited in the sierra is the belief that the souls of the dead go to a land called Upamarca, which can be explained as the silent land, or land of the dumb.[1] As the poetic Latin phrase has it, *Regio silentium.* They say that before reaching it, they come to a broad river which must be crossed on a slender bridge made of human hair. Others say they will encounter a pack of black dogs, and in some localities they raise such dogs and kill them for fear of this superstition.[2] Still others hold to a tradition that the souls of the dead go where the huacas are. The people of the town of Huacho, and other towns on the coast, say that they go to the isle of guano and that the sea lions, which they call *tumi,* carry them there.

They know no happiness in this life or in the other besides having a good farm to give them food and drink. They say that at death they go to the beyond to work their farms and sow their seeds. They do not believe there will be punishment there for the wicked nor glory for the good. They are persuaded that the dead feel, eat, and drink, and only with great pain can they be buried and bound to earth. In their machays and burial places in the fields, where they are not interred, but placed in a small hollow or cave or little house, they have more rest. This is why they try to remove bodies from the church, for, deceived as they are by these errors, they have no knowledge of the resurrection of the body.

Similarly, they have no knowledge of nor esteem for the sacraments such as the Eucharist and Penance. All but a few of those examined by the visitor say that they have always kept silent during the sacramental confession concerning the adoration of huacas, the consulting of sorcerers, and other sins of idolatry. At the beginning of the visit I was astonished at this, and wishing to find out whether their silence about such sins was purely and simply ignorance or whether it implied

---

[1] *Upa* means mute; *marca,* region. Cieza de León, *Señorío de los incas,* Chap. III. Also Garcilaso, Acosta, Betanzos, Ondegardo, and Cobo.

[2] Calancha, *Crónica moralizada,* Bk. II, Chap. XII, p. 379. *El Perú— bocetos históricos,* 2nd Series, p. 67.

malice, I questioned an Indian in the presence of the visitor. He had told what huacas he worshiped, and I asked him whether he had confessed this sin to the priest and he said no. So I questioned him again, using this phrase in his language:

"What did your heart say when you kept silent about these sins?"

His reply was to burst out crying, groaning, and sobbing and when he was able to talk, he said:

"My heart told me I was deceiving God and the priest."

And he said this with such feeling that for a long time he would not leave the church and go into the cemetery where the other Indians were but remained in a corner weeping after he had moved away from us.

No small cause for their having neither knowledge of nor a proper esteem for the confession is the little opportunity for it that some of their priests have given them. They not only fail to exhort them to confession during the year but regard it as an impertinence to admit them to it even when, because of their piety, some of them wish to confess.

Greater still are their forgetfulness and their ignorance of the Most Blessed Sacrament of the Altar, for even though in some localities priests who are conscientious about the well-being of the Indians have been diligent in providing this sacrament for them, so that they may take Communion at Easter, the fact is that they generally do not take Communion even then. Nor do they take it by means of the viaticum when they are ill, because the priest, since he wants to avoid the trouble of providing it, says they are incapable of it. Yet this is one of the mysteries of our faith, and I believe that one of the reasons why they are not deeply grounded in it and rooted in it is that the sacrament is not offered to them. I need no other basis for this than the word and testimony of the Supreme Pontiff and Vicar of Christ Our Lord. While I was in Rome, Clement VIII, of happy memory, asked about this country in these words:

"*Quomodo se habent indi Peruani circa religionem Christianam?*"

And replying to His Holiness the answer was given that in many places they still retained and worshiped their huacas and idols. To this His Holiness replied:

"Communicant in Paschate?"

He was answered that very few of them take Communion and that generally they do not, to which the Supreme Pontiff replied:

"Non erunt vere Christiani, donec communicent in Paschate."

As the experience and teaching of the saints and especially that of glorious Saint Augustine has shown, the ornaments and trappings of divine worship are of no little value, particularly in helping the common people to appreciate the things of Christianity. And since the Indians are generally inclined to the veneration and worship of God, it is easy to see how little help they receive in certain places to enable them to acquire an esteem for and knowledge of the true religion; this is shown by neglect of the external ornamentation of their churches and the celebration of the divine offices. I could name a very large town where no mass has ever been sung except on the day of the Vocation of the Church, and then only by the efforts of the Indians, who bring their singers from afar off to officiate at mass. In that town there is no one who knows how to read or to assist at mass except a single Indian, and he badly. I asked the priest why he had not established a school, which would have been easy and profitable to do, in which they might have learned to read and to sing, for it would have been profitable to them to perform chanted masses and he replied that the Indians did not need to read or write, since such knowledge would be of no use to them except to criticize their priests.[3]

---

[3] The argument is without foundation unless it first be proved that unfortunate Indians did not suffer from the abuse by their priests and that in most cases they were not stimulated toward goodness by the good example of their pastors, and this was precisely what often happened.

CHAPTER EIGHT

Other Causes of the Idolatry of the Indians

A NOTHER contributory cause of Indian idolatry is the large number of ministers and teachers thereof that they have among them, a fact to be inferred from the cases discovered and punished in the towns. If a reckoning is made of all the greater and lesser ministers, we generally find one minister or teacher for every ten Indians or less. Each clan and faction has its own priests, and even when no more than three or four houses are left in a clan, they have their huaca and a priest to guard it. I saw one clan composed of but a single Indian and his wife, and the priesthood for the huaca of the clan had been entrusted to him. From this it is easy to understand why, with so many teachers of idolatry among them and the constant reiteration on every occasion of doctrines learned in childhood—doctrines altogether suited to their capacity and inclination—the Indians are well instructed and well practiced in the rites of paganism. Contrast this with the fact that there is no one to teach them the mysteries of our faith, mysteries far above their comprehension. The saying "late, bad, and never"[a] seems to apply. Thus we find the Indians almost totally ignorant of the Christian religion. I could name a town of about three hundred and fifty confessed Christians where, within an hour of our arrival, the people came of their own free will to denounce some thirty sorcerers. And the number soon reached forty. They had not seen a priest in four or five months, and when he did come it was for a few days only, after which he returned to his other town, a small one, because it had a better church. Is it then very astonishing that idolatry persists where the priest comes so

[a] There is no good equivalent saying in English. The gist appears to be that Christianity is taught belatedly, badly, or never, in contrast with the Indians' never-ending instruction in paganism.

infrequently and in such haste, and where there are so many well-established ministers and teachers of idolatry?

To the continued presence of the sorcerers another reason for the preservation of idolatry among the Indians can be added. This is the freedom of action allowed the caciques and curacas, their care and solicitude in honoring and maintaining the sorcerers, in hiding the huacas, in celebrating the festivals, in knowing the traditions and fables of their ancestors, and in telling and teaching them to the rest. For if the caciques were what they ought to be, they could find a simple way of getting rid of idolatry. As it is, they do as they please with the Indians, and if they want them to be idolatrous they are idolatrous, if they want them to be Christians they will be Christians. They have no will apart from their caciques, who are a model for them in everything that they do.

Another reason is the failure to take the movable huacas out of their sight, for this would have been one means of uprooting them from their hearts also. Not only every town but every clan and faction, however small, has them. As I have already remarked, it was a mistake not to have burned the munaos of the lowlands, which are called malquis in the sierra, for the Indians esteem them more than their huacas; a mistake not to have destroyed their machays, or burial places of their grandfathers and progenitors to which they carry the bodies stolen from the church; a mistake not to have deprived them of their *morpis,* as they call them in the lowlands, or chancas, as they say in Cuzco, or conopas, as they are called in this archbishopric, which are their household gods, passed on from father to son as the richest and most precious of their few jewels. Rare are those who do not have them, for they are the principal inheritance of the family, and sometimes they have two, three, or four of them.

A cacique I know freely showed me eleven conopas, and his wife five, each with its own name. Furthermore, up to now no notice has been taken of their ancient shirts of cumbi, which they offer to their huacas and with which they dress up their malquis, or which they put on at festival time or during the sacrifices to the huacas.

They have been allowed to keep their half-moons of silver, called chacrahinca; the objects called huamas; and others like diadems or round plates which they call tincurpa, some of which are of copper, some of silver, and not a few of gold; the shirts overlaid with silver and the huaracas they wear upon their heads with silver buttons and plumes of various colors; and the *huacras,* which are like necklaces or high collars of various colors. All these, as noted above, are ornaments of the huacas and are used for festivals only. This does not mean that all the shirts of cumbi must be taken away from them with the excuse that they belong to the huacas, but only those which have been worn by their malquis or huacas and which were used solely for this ministry. It would be preferable to burn the last-mentioned and not to keep them, for the Indians cannot understand being deprived of these things and then seeing them preserved.

Nor had it been observed that they owned various instruments used to summon the people for the festivals and celebrations of the huacas, such as the many ancient trumpets of copper or silver, of different shape and appearance from ours, the great coiled horns which they play, called *antari* and *pututu,* and other instruments called *pincollos,* which are bone or cane flutes. For the festivals of the huacas they also have, in addition to the foregoing, antlers and horns of mountain goats, gourds and drinking vessels made from horn, and many other vessels for drinking in addition to the *aquillas*[b] of silver, wood, or clay, in many forms and shapes. Nor was any attention paid to the quantity of small drums used to accompany their drunkenness. Even less noticed were the offices and costumes of the parianas, of which we have already spoken.

Far from being hidden, all these objects were used publicly and carried in their festivals and dances in full view of the Spaniards and priests; we have often seen them within the Cercado de Lima. It is also a well-known and a well-established fact that in many localities, with the pretext of the

[b] *Aquilla* or *kero (quero).* An Inca drinking vessel. Many of them are still preserved. They range from simple, painted clay tumblers to hardwood vessels inlaid with silver and decorated with elaborate scenes.

festival of Corpus Christi, they celebrate the festival of Oncoymita which, as we have said, occurs at about the same time. In the province of Chinchacocha, when it was visited, it was discovered that they carried in the procession two live llamas on a raised platform as a part of a festival and dance. It was also learned that these animals were really intended as offerings and sacrifices to two lagoons called Urcococha and Choclococha, which is where they say llamas come from and have their origin. The dissimulation and boldness of the Indians has also reached such a point that during the feast of the Corpus they have slyly hidden a small huaca on the very platform of the monstrance of the Holy Sacrament. And a priest told me that he found huacas in the hollow niches of the saints in front of the holy altar, and others below the altar, placed there by the sacristan. I have also seen them behind the church. It was discovered in Haurochirí by Dr. Francisco de Avila that in order to worship an idol in the form of a woman called Chupixamor, and Mamayoc, they celebrated a festival to the image of Our Lady of the Assumption, and to worship a male idol by the name of Huayhuay, they celebrated a festival to a crucifix.

No one who saw them performing these celebrations thought there was any malice in it but considered them pastimes, traditional dances, and so forth. If the Indians were thereby indulging in vain superstitions, the fact hardly needed to be noticed. In like fashion, no attention was paid to their names or surnames which were those of the huacas or malquis, used for superstitious reasons, as we have noted with regard to the chuchus, or twins, and the chacpas, or children born feet first, since even such children have special names.

The fact that these activities were passed over and little or no notice was taken of them has led the Indians to keep them up and perform them with impunity. There has been even more carelessness and laxity in consenting to and glossing over their drunkenness when they assemble in the fields, especially during the *mingas*,[c] when they come together to build a house

[c] Cooperative labor.

or to farm. It is their custom to do everything by community effort and the common bond of such groups is to drink until they fall down. It is from these sources in addition to incest and many other wicked practices that the idolatry of past centuries has arisen.

Thus do many interpret the book of Exodus, which says *sedit populus manducare, et bibere, et surrexit ludere,* which was to worship the golden calf, and so the priests overlook their conduct as an incurable ill without hope of remedy. They say they do not wish to have anything to do with drunken Indians. I have seen towns where the tithe intended for the purchase of medicine is spent on wine. They[d] used to send a certain number of bottles to a town, and a like quantity to another, and it was a very bad and very high-priced wine, as I was told by a curate who sampled it in my presence. If they had also sent oil, it might have been said that they were acting like the Samaritan of the Gospel. They would like to see all diseases treated with wine, for that is a profitable business for them. Not everyone is guilty of these practices, but most of them are.

I could show a note which came into my possession in which the lieutenant of a political faction wrote to the cacique of a town as follows:

"Brother X, I am sending you today a certain number of bottles of wine. See to it that they are sold in so many days and at such and such a price. Since I look after your business, look after mine."

Such collusion, which the priests and *corregidors* must amend, and the Indians' awareness of its existence are another reason why the Indians have no idea of the miserable state they are in. For it is usual with persons of limited understanding to know and estimate guilt not in and of itself, but by the punishment it receives. They observe that when they are caught, as they frequently are, in their drunkenness, superstitions, and idolatries, they have either not been punished at

[d] Probably a reference to Spanish merchants, but Father Arriaga does not specify.

all, or the punishment has been light. They see further, as I have already observed, and as Father Joseph Acosta also remarks in Chapter 19, Book 4, of his *De procurando salute Indorum,* that they are punished severely for unimportant offenses, such as not fetching something as quickly as they are expected to, or for losing or breaking something they are sent for, and such like minor infractions. But when their adultery and idolatry are glossed over, they come to regard the sins which go unpunished as minor ones and less important than those they are punished for. On many occasions they have been guilty only of forgetfulness or the natural carelessness of the Indian and have deserved no punishment at all.

Aside from these extrinsic causes which serve to foment and preserve idolatry among the Indians, there are two others that are intrinsic, two errors by which the Devil and his ministers have persuaded and blinded the Indians. The first is the belief and conviction that what the fathers preach is the truth, that the God of the Spaniards is a good God, but that this teaching is meaningful for the Viracochas and Spaniards only, whereas the huacas and malquis are intended for the Indians, together with the festivals and everything else that their ancestors, old men, and sorcerers have taught them. This is a common conviction among the Indians, oft repeated by their sorcerers, that the statues of the saints represent the huacas of the Viracochas, and that as they have theirs, the Indians have theirs also. And this deception and error is most harmful.

An even more common error than the previous one is their tendency to carry water on both shoulders, to have recourse to both religions at once. I know a place where a cloak was made for the image of Our Lady and a shirt for their huaca from the same cloth. They feel and even say that they can worship their huacas while believing in God the Father, Son, and Holy Ghost. Thus, for the worship of Jesus Christ they generally offer what they offer their huacas. They celebrate their festivals for Him and go to church, hear mass, and even take Communion. However, in this last matter the Lord has instilled some awe in them and so lofty a notion of the sacra-

ment, that some of those who are able to do so do not take
it when it is offered. Only persons well instructed in the
mysteries of our faith and undeceived of their errors ask permission to take Communion. Most of the Indians have not
yet had their huacas and conopas taken away from them,
their festivals disturbed, nor their abuses and superstitions
punished, and so they think their lies compatible with our
truth and their idolatry with our faith. Dagon is their Ark,
and Christ their Baal. They are punctilious like the Samaritans
of the Holy Scriptures in the fourth book of Kings, Chapter 17:
*qui cum Dominum colerent, Diis quoque suis serviebant iuxta
consuetudinem gentium.* After relating their errors the Sacred
Text concludes: *Fuerunt igitur gentes ista timentes Dominum,
sed nihilominus, et idolis suis servientes, nam et filii eorum et
nepotes sicut fecerunt patres sui, ita faciunt usque in presentem
diem.*

Such is the miserable state of the Indians now being visited.
These are the huacas they worship, the ministers thereof,
their offerings and festivals, the abuses and superstitions
they practice, and the causes I have been able to ascertain
for the evils and miseries in which they find themselves.

I do not believe it would be difficult to prove that this
pestilence is common to the whole kingdom, although it is
possible to hope that there is little or no idolatry in a few
places where Christian doctrine has been watered and cultivated. We can note the difference between the Valley of
Xauja, where the missions of the Dominicans and Franciscans
are, where the Indians receive constant care and teaching,
where divine worship is properly performed with music and
ceremony, and where all possible means are employed for the
teaching of the Indians, and the towns that are neglected.
Thus, one realizes that there was no less evil elsewhere than
in the towns that are now being visited, for evil exists in both
places, and for the same reason. Yet some astonishment was
expressed and doubts were raised, until experience removed
doubt, concerning the existence of idolatry among the Indians,
because the Archbishop had quite frequently visited the towns

in person, and the holy prelate, Don Toribio, who is now in glory, had shown equal zeal, omitting no town, however small or distant. Yet nothing was discovered nor found out, so closely was the secret kept.

Perhaps what could not then be achieved by all the effort then expended has now been accomplished through Don Toribio's intercession as he enjoys the presence of Our Lord in heaven and prays for life and health for His Illustrious Lordship who now governs, so that, employing all possible means, this pestilence may be done away with in the whole archbishopric. And this is being accomplished through the favor of the Lord Our God. But before we seek remedies for these evils, let us see what truth there is in the two suppositions that I have frequently touched upon.

CHAPTER NINE

Proving That in the Provinces Not Yet Visited Much Idolatry Remains

THE FIRST of my two suppositions is that in the provinces not yet visited, there is as much idolatry as in those already visited. The second is that in those visited, many traces and roots of idolatry yet remain. And as the one supposition is as sure as the other, and both are true as such, like principles *per se notos,* I have desisted from trying to prove them. But because I know that some persons in great authority doubt what has been said, despite the evidence that makes it plain, as specified in previous chapters, I will add the weight of some persons worthy of credence, whose letters I have received since I began to print this work. I shall present them just as they were written, without adding a word. Let the first be that of Father Luis de Teruel, of our Society, who was one of the three who went with us on the visit with

Dr. Hernando de Avendaño. After leaving the city of Lima for Chuquisaca, 300 leagues away, he wrote at the half way point, from Cuzco, as follows:

From Huamanga I wrote your Reverence to urge haste in printing the instructions for visits relating to idolatry. They are much needed and must be done properly, for although the fathers of the school who went out with the visitor found much idolatry, this was as nothing in comparison with the whole of it. As Dr. Avila passed by, he found easily so many traces of idolatry that if he had gone forth only to deal with what remained, his time would have been well spent. Let your Reverence laugh if he hears it said that there are towns which do not need visiting, for ever since we left Lima, Father Pablo de Paredes and I have been preaching and hearing confession in the towns and in some of the *tambos,*[a] omitting the whole district of Huarochirí, which ought to be visited again very shortly. In Xauxa the friars and some of the Spaniards told us about some thousand cases of backsliding. But the need is greatest in Huamanga, where the two of us preached sermons during the entire week that we were there. In that city there are so many sorcerers, called *licenciados,* so many conopas, huacanquis, and the like, that hardly anyone fails to know about them. In Andahuaylas we heard about a very famous and evil female *licenciada.* In Uramarca another good old man told me that when someone dies, they bury him in new clothes and offer him food, and every year the offering is renewed. He told us also that they keep the bodies of their pagan ancestors in caves and ancient tombs and make sacrifices to them as they begin to work the ground for sowing, while they make chicha on the farms. If a fire sparks, they say the souls of their ancestors are thirsty and hungry, and they throw corn and chicha and potatoes and other foods into the fire for them to eat and drink. They also sacrifice in the same way when they are ill. We were only there one afternoon and the following night, and so I was not able to get any more information out of the old men about the huacas, except that such and such a one, which he named, used to be worshiped but is not worshiped anymore. This is a common answer in all the towns I have visited. We preached against this practice during the afternoon, and on

---

[a] *Tambo,* a Quechua word. This was a rest or relay stop on the Inca messenger routes. These posts were stocked with provisions.

the following morning, which was Sunday, we confessed a few persons. We could not accommodate them all, although they asked for it, as we did not wish to lose a day. In Huancaraime we rested a day, made a procession, and taught. We also preached a sermon against huacas and sorcerers in general, for we had no specific information except to the effect that they washed the bodies of the dead, dressed them up, and stayed up all night in drunkenness. As a result, they confessed these two offenses all day until a good while after prayers, and some of them made general confessions to the glory of the Lord Our God. Three famous sorceresses, although old and deaf, came forward. The principal worship in this town is of malquis, or the mummies of their ancestors, of which they say there is a great abundance. They also practice divination of future events, using guinea pigs and spiders.

When someone dies they get very drunk and stay up all night singing the praise of the dead. After the burial they wash in a certain stream agreed upon for the purpose and burn the dead person's old clothes. Then in the days immediately following, if the fire happens to spark, or an owl hoots, or a hawk cries out over the dead man's house, they say he is hungry and cold, and they burn corn and potatoes for him. Little by little they also burn his ornaments until there are none left. There is also an ancient huaca here, the name of which I forget, that used to talk in the time of the Incas.[1] There is a tradition about it that when Manco Cápac was passing through the town, he went to it to offer a sacrifice and it told him that it would not receive him because he was not the legitimate Inca, and it told him to leave the kingdom. At this Manco Cápac became very angry and had the huaca thrown down the hill. When they went to move the stone, a brightly colored parrot came out of it and flew up the hill. And although the Inca commanded the people of the town to follow it and throw stones at it, they could not hit it before it reached another stone, and this stone split open and shut the parrot up inside and then became whole again. And these two stones that the parrot came out of and went into were huge. Some years ago a virtuous Indian of this town, a member of our Society in Cuzco, wished to set up some crosses on the hill where the stones are; although the Indians tried to frighten him off, he went up with his crosses, and a great wind came up and a noise so loud that it sounded like talking. He was

---

[1] This was the huaca *Huarihuilca* or *Huarivilca*.

very frightened, and his hair, so he told us, stood on end. But invoking the name of JESUS, he concluded his devotions. Then the wind blew so hard that the crosses broke, and although they were set up again they broke a second time. He told me that that kind of gusts do not generally occur in that area.

When they start to sow they make sacrifices to their household gods. They throw white corn on them and after a few days they pick it up and sow it, and they say this brings a good crop. When they are ill, their sorcerers tell them to throw white corn on the highway so that passersby will carry away their illness. At other times, the sorcerer goes to the top of the nearest hill and makes a point of throwing stones at it with his slingshot, complaining that it has been the cause of an illness, which he begs it to take away. For the same purpose they wash the sick person with chicha and rub him with white corn. We have also found many other things on the road that would take too long to tell, and surely they are a proof of the blindness in which these people live and of their need for help. When we came back we had news of the Provinces of Aymaraes, Cotabambas, and Condesuyos in Arequipa, which are like an uncultivated forest, where it seems as if the faith of Jesus Christ has never been preached.

The letter goes on, but this is enough to show that the whole cloth is made from the same wool, is of the same color, and has the same spots which will not come out the first time it is washed. This can also be seen in a part of another letter from a secular priest, a truthful man, zealous of the glory of Our Lord and the good of the Indians. His letter was addressed to the visitor, Dr. Diego Ramírez Cura, who is presently a member of the chapter of this city, asking him as an experienced man for instructions as to how to uproot idolatry in the towns where he was situated, two hundred leagues from this city. This is what he says:

I am making my presence felt here, and I am helped by your Grace's two letters of instruction giving details as to the ceremonies, the abuses, the divinations, the tricks, and deceptions of the Indian priests, how they pretend to say mass, confess, cure and dogmatize, and make themselves prophets of things to come, not to mention their rites and worship, for everyone agrees as to what is going on. The infirmity of these unfortunate people is general, though more pronounced in the vicinity of Potosí, where this accursed pestilence rages at its height. The reason for this is that justice seeks its own profit only, the priests stay at the foot of the altar and dare not denounce or get rid of the evils they have noticed, not even the mixture of our holy ceremonies with their Indian rites on behalf of the dead during the week of All Saints. From this country to Charcas (a distance of more than a hundred leagues, and one of the most populous and well frequented regions of all Peru) the faith has not been planted, for the ways of the people reflect indifference and haughtiness, with no hint of devotion. They seem rather to feel hatred and enmity and have a bad attitude toward God. In this they are almost justified, because we who teach them appear to demonstrate that growing rich quickly is our principal aim. This must be to the detriment of the flock, for they are shorn without piety or love. The treatment they receive from the Spaniards and the *corregidors* is cruel and unpalatable, and so they leave their towns and wander about and do not let their priests and pastors get to know them. For this reason there are churches to be built, others that have fallen down, and some in bad repair, and without ornaments. There are isolated towns where no one has paid taxes to His Majesty except poor women, and I declare that there are in this province today more than two thousand widows paying taxes for husbands who have been dead for ten years, and there are even more whose husbands have been dead for five years or less.

This is a passage from the abovementioned letter.

The illustrious Dr. Don Pedro de Valencia, bishop of Chuquiavo, who was promoted to his see from the post of chanter of this one, because of his experience in this archbishopric and because of the zeal Our Lord has given him for the good of his flock, entrusted the visit concerning idolatry to a priest of much excellence. A few days after the visit began, this priest wrote the following letter, which His Lordship sent to me to be shown to the Viceroy:

I wish to advise Your Lordship of my labors against the Indian sorcerers, and principally against a most abominable stone idol about six yards high which I discovered two leagues from this town of Hilavi. It stood on the highest hill in the region, on a slope that faces the rising sun. At the foot of the hill, in a small wood, are the huts of the Indians who guard it. There are also many ancient and extensive Indian burial niches, elaborately contrived of interlocking stones, which they identify as the former leaders of the town of Hilavi. A little clearing had been hacked out and in it stood a carved stone statue representing two monstrous figures, one of a man looking toward the rising sun. Back-to-back with him was another with the face of a woman, facing toward the setting sun. From the feet of these figures are great snakes rising toward their heads, one on the right and one on the left, along with other carvings representing toads. This huaca was uncovered from the breast to the head; the rest of it was below ground.[2] It took thirty persons three days to uncover the site around the idol, and they found on both sides, in front of the two faces, well-placed square stones about a palm and a half high, serving apparently as sacrifice stones or altars. After pulling these idols off their foundations, we found fine sheets of gold where the altar had been. They lay scattered about and sparkled in the sun. It required much effort on my part to remove this idol and to destroy it, and much more effort to disillusion the Indians. But what grieves me most at present, Illustrious Lord, is that my diligence, and the warnings and preaching that I offer this town, in order to provide Christian teaching, to disillusion the Indians, and make them cease their concubinage, incest, and other vices, do not have the effect that I desire. The fact is that the people, living as they do on scattered farms in the deep valleys, seldom come together. And the one who supports this disorder is a rascally head cacique. It is public knowledge that he orders the Indians not to attend mass nor to go to Christian teaching. Instead, he keeps many of them busy working his lands, tending his flocks, and doing other work. Such is the scandalous way he lives. He has not confessed for many years, and I can think of no remedy for his conduct. I shall do what I can, but Your Lordship should be forewarned in case those who are punished should present themselves with complaints, and so forth.

[2] Copies of this hermaphrodite idol may be seen in the museum of Peruvian antiquities of Dr. Javier Prado in Lima. The idols are of silver and were taken from among the huacas of Pachacámac and from the region of Lake Titicaca.

Thus writes the visitor, Alonso García Quadrado. The visitor Bartolomé de Dueñas, writing from Tiahuánaco, says even more, but this I shall omit in the interest of brevity.

CHAPTER TEN

Showing That in the Provinces That Have Been Visited Many Roots of Idolatry Remain

IT HAS BEEN sufficiently proved by what has been said that no less idolatry remains in the other provinces of the kingdom than was found in those of this archbishopric. Let us now see whether it is not just as true that the tangled growth and roots of idolatry cannot be removed by that preliminary plowing which is performed during the first visit. Sufficient testimony on this point can be found in the letters and reports sent this past week to the Lord Viceroy and Lord Archbishop of this city by Licentiate Rodrigo Hernández Príncipe. This priest served the mission of Santo Domingo de Ocros, in the *corregidor* district of Cajatambo, but Our Lord made him wish to leave there and, with the permission of the Lord Viceroy and the Lord Archbishop, to travel through the towns of his district without the title or office of visitor, catechizing, preaching, and confessing, employing in his work that good talent which Our Lord has given him. He took with him as his only companion a good lame Indian, who went with us on our visit, a man as well informed in the matters of our Holy Faith as he is a diligent observer of the superstitions of the Indians. He catechizes admirably for both reasons.

In the course of this mission, which is still in progress, Licentiate Príncipe has rendered and continues to render great service to Our Lord through the means and intercession of the blessed Virgin Mary, whom he has taken for his advocate in this enterprise. All the towns that he has passed through are left undeceived of their errors and encóuraged in the service of Our Lord, and their churches are repaired as regards ornaments and images. From every town he sends back money for this purpose. I have this very day money he has sent to buy what is needed for the churches of four towns. With his own money, sent to me for the purpose, I have bought and sent out to him many rosaries, which he distributes among the Indians. But let us now see in more detail something of what he has accomplished by reading from one of his letters, which I personally delivered to the Lord Prince of Esquilache, viceroy of the kingdom. He begins thus:

I sent to Lima to obtain approval for a Brotherhood of Our Lady of Loreto, which was founded in Totopon[1] as an act of gratitude for the intervention of the Serene Queen of the Angels in the discovery of the idols and the Christianization of these Indians. I then came upon a second town, that of Cahacay, where I continued as I had begun, preaching morning and evening and catechizing them in the rudiments of the faith, declaring that my coming was solely to disenchant them of the error of idolatry, serving the Lord in that way, as his prelates desired. The town was impressed by an informal talk Friday night during the teaching of Christian doctrine, and this was preceded by a general fast to make the town ready. That very night after my talk some Indians came up with a great show of grief and repentance to say that although they had not presently been idolatrous and gone to their huacas since the visit, as they used to, nevertheless they had continued to worship them in their hearts, and in their houses and farms, with both inward and outward signs. By the urging of the Devil they had been persuaded that after this time another would come when they could safely return to their ancient ways, amid the indifference of their pastors. For this reason, they had not revealed everything about their huacas but had merely pointed out some which they had purposely placed on the surface of the ground together with utensils for their use; fearing a holocaust, like that which the astute Friar Francisco had made, they said that their own huacas, bequeathed to them by their ancestors, had been buried two or more yards underground in the very places where the crosses of the previous

[1] Totopon, in Spain.

visit were. To demonstrate the truth of this assertion they said they would take me to see all this with my own eyes, for God was already giving his mercy to cure their blindness.

Another day, a Saturday, after having said the mass of Our Lady, praying that She might give us success, as everyone in the town had already become a slave of the Mother of God according to the charter of brotherhood, we walked to the old town, a league and a half away by roads so rough we could hardly proceed, even on foot.

The first town was Choquechuco where, when we had dug down about two yards deep where the cross was, we brought out the huaca of the town. It was of liver-colored stone with a face and eyes and stood upon a stone base with twenty-five conopas, or lesser idols, around it. For an offering it had a lot of big and little silver pieces and other utensils for sacrifices.

In the lowlands, in the town of Humi,[2] there was a cross where the huaca Humivilca had been removed at the time of the visit. We dug down about two yards at that point and came upon an Indian stone idol, and near it another russet-colored stone which they call his brother. Both were seated on a flat stone with thirty-two conopas and many sacrifices around them.

In the town of Quichumarca, at the place where the cross had been during the previous visit, we again dug down about three yards, and we were about to give up when we came upon the evidence of sacrifices and three huacas. The largest they call Huari Huaca, and with him were his two brothers, with such strange faces that they were horrifying to look at. There were also forty-seven conopas, and among the sacrifices were pieces of silver, a copper trumpet with a silver mouthpiece, and three large stones, two of them worn with time.

From there we went to the town of Chochas where in a narrow defile stood a towering crag with a cross on top of it. From this place they said they had removed the huaca which was taken to the visitor. But I was determined to climb up the crag guided by the old men, using a winding path in lieu of a staircase. But I could not go more than halfway up, for it seemed reckless to go any further. The Indians went on up with no little effort and brought me back the huaca of Llaxavilca, which was like half a body, head

---

[2] All the towns mentioned in this chapter belong to the former *corregidor* district of Huaylas, now in the department of Ancash.

down and with one eye larger than the other. Close by was another huaca. Both were sitting on a flat stone, and there were bones all around from the sacrifice of llamas.

All the malquis (or pagan mummies which the Indians worship), of which we found a great many, we burned. Among them were two pairs of small silver tumblers which the Indians seem to have used to give the dead a drink. When night had fallen we came back, thanking the Lord for our success and bringing all the idols and other things which we had found. On the following day, a Sunday, we celebrated the festival of the Mother of God and made a solemn procession, attributing our find to her intercession. Licentiate Francisco de Virves, the priest of this mission, who had helped us like a good pastor, did the preaching. The public was most devout and begged me to found a Brotherhood of the Vocation of Our Lady, which I did.

This same day, on the festival of Our Lady, they told me of the location of another huaca and I went there personally, for I think these exercises, in which gold is not being sought but the salvation of souls, are most entertaining. We went to Chanca, which we had not heard of on the previous visit. After a short walk around the old town we came upon the famous huaca, already mentioned, named Sañumama.[a] It was in the form of an ancient jug or jar and with it were drinking vessels of clay like those in Cuzco, all of them buried underground in a kind of storehouse. On the door frame were two *llampis* of clay with which they drink toasts to the huaca. In the midst of the pottery there were three large jars, and the middle one, which was the huaca, was full of chicha up to its neck, for since time immemorial they had been throwing chicha into it and it had been turning into water. This water was full of sacrifices of guinea pigs and other things used in this devilish ministry. They say that on Corpus Christi Day they gave it festive treatment, taking it out of its place and drinking toasts to it in the town. They dress it up in a mantle with its silver clasps. And this huaca was venerated in all the surrounding provinces.

The female companion of this huaca, Mamasañu, was some distance away. Digging about a yard, we came upon ashes and the burned remnants of many bones and sacrifices, many idols without heads and with their legs broken; the idol was in the middle of a large stone, resting upon a large sheet of lead, with a great many conopas

---

[a] An error. This huaca has not been mentioned previously.

nearby. I learned that these idols had been burned by Fray Francisco, of whom I have spoken, and that after his departure the Indians had buried them there with the huaca. All this material was taken to town and, in the presence of everyone, we built a great bonfire and burned everything and threw the ashes into a ditch so that the Devil might not join them together again.

In the town of Chuquimarca, three leagues east of Cahacay, we took out the huaca Quénac, which was about forty-five inches tall, with the face of an Indian. They say that they took his brother to the visitor, but this one was buried deeper with his sacrifices.

In the ancient town of Huahalla, not far from this one, we dug up an armless stone giant. The whole body was buried with only the head protruding, and the latter was well covered with flagstones. The old men of the clan say of this huaca, which is called Huari, and also Chani, that they used to give it chewed coca by placing it in his mouth. From another place we removed two whole mummies, called Caxapárac and his son Huaratama, which were famous and highly respected by everyone. They rested in their burial places, decked out as if for war, with plumage of various colors and dressed in garments which had become worn with time. A little way away was another mummy in storage, dressed like the others, and called Vinchos.

All these mummies and huacas were burned to the applause and pleasure of everyone. And it is remarkable that the very old men and women who are the hiders and guardians of the huacas should have brought them to me, saying,

"My Father, burn them, these are the demons that have done us so much harm."

This account is from the letter which was given to His Excellency concerning the discoveries made in the single town of Cahacay, subsequent to the visit. One can infer from this the care that the Indians have taken to hide their huacas, and the diligence and effort that it costs to discover them. And we may come to understand thereby what the patience, suffering, and efficacy of the Word of God can accomplish. By it the priests may be inspired to do their duty, that is to preach and catechize frequently and truly and with a desire to convince the Indians, disenchanting them of the lies they have learned and teaching them the truth of which they are ignorant. For others are being aroused through charity to follow the example of Licentiate Rodrigo Hernández. And although it is long, it is not irrelevant, and so I will quote another letter of his, written to the Lord Archbishop on the same subject, which reads as follows:

In the year 1575 a Dominican father named Friar Francisco burned and destroyed many huacas throughout this province. As he was inexperienced in Indian affairs and had a great deal to do, he moved about quickly and did not notice all the huacas, and so the Indians took the precaution of hiding them. They were also careful to preserve the pieces of the broken and half-burned huacas. For, as I shall now explain, the respect, love, and fear which the Devil inspires in them is astonishing to see. The fact is that the old men say of their own free will and impulse, when they have been disillusioned, that the Devil had blinded them and that we ought to go and remove the huacas from their hiding places. But when we go, taking them for guides, they proceed as unwillingly as if they were going to their own execution or beheading, trembling, perspiring, and biting their tongues so that they can hardly talk or move their hands and feet. For I think the Devil reminds them of the tender love they have felt for their huacas, the care with which they have guarded them, and the grief they will feel if they are deprived of them. Thus we do the work of the Lord, going sometimes blindly about in one cart or another, from one storehouse to another, but mostly on foot, and enduring the rigor of the sun and air and undergoing frequent changes of climate, some hot, some cold, until Our Lord is served and His Mother is blessed (for it is She who inspires this work), until the hour of pure persuasion and urging is reached. And though our work is occasionally done with threats and loss of patience, most of the time our discoveries are made through the kindness prescribed in the Gospel, since the great and difficult was never easy, especially in the salvation of souls.

Above the town of Yámor we removed the huaca Líbiac, or lightning, which was a huge stone cleft in two by a bolt of lightning, and around it was an abundance of sacrifices of llamas and other things.

On top of a hill was the huaca Quénac, surrounded by many

stones. It had an Indian face but had no arms or feet, and it was buried about a yard deep along with many sacrifices and a copper trumpet used to call the people together for their festivals.

In the midst of these buildings and fortresses of the ancient town they brought to the visitor a huaca which was on the surface of the ground, called Huair Yurac, son of Apu Yurac. They had told the visitor that this idol had been burned by Friar Francisco, but they assured me that he had turned into a falcon, that he had sons, and that this falcon was to be found in this place. I ordered them to start digging, and at a depth of about two yards we came upon a storage place in a kind of cave where there was a stone falcon sitting on a little sheet of silver surrounded by many conopas, representing the huaca's servants. There were also many sacrifices and a trumpet. Nearby were four whole mummies, with plumes and rich garments, though worn with time. They call these the sons of the huaca and the progenitors of the clan, and so they worshiped them and consulted them whenever they deemed it necessary. These mummies are more harmful than the huacas, because the worship of the latter takes place once a year, whereas the dead are worshiped every day.

About a league from town, on the road to Cahacay, we found the huaca Quénac Vilca, a fierce looking stone idol, surrounded by a lot of small pieces of silver and sea shells. The visitor had burned this idol's son, called Huayna Quénac. In the house of the parents of a leading Indian they had hidden the hair of a great-grandfather, an Indian idolater. These locks of hair were displayed, respected, and worshiped in his memory. Friar Francisco burned this mummy, because they had greatly respected him in life as one of the advisers of the Inca.

In the ancient town of Hupa, in a stronghold of cut stone, we dug down more than two and a half yards and found a little house made of ashlars in which was the huaca Apu Yurac, carved from stone and with an Indian face. It was about three-quarters normal height, resting on silver sheets, surrounded by many conopas and sacrifices, and with a trumpet and various other instruments used in the festivals.

In addition to this huaca we removed the huaca Achcay, which looked like the first one. In both places we set up crosses and celebrated a festival to Our Lady and Patroness. And because the Indians had been incredulous about the existence of purgatory, I catechized them about it, and since they urged me to found a Brotherhood of the Souls of Purgatory, I did so.

The priest and I spent four days in Huaylla Cayan catechizing and preaching, but I felt strongly impelled to go first to the town of Colqueyoc, which is four leagues away on a very bad road. Before I left for Cahacay I had spent four days there but was chagrined to perceive that there was little likelihood of success, and because I had not seen their priest to get his permission, I left for the time being. But now I thought I would go back and satisfy my conscience. I went to the town with the priest and we spent a week in catechisms, sermons, and in refuting their errors. Finally I told the people that I found them harsh and impious and that I felt that a great impediment was making them so. This was their keeping their huacas and living in paganism. Thereat the Lord moved them deeply, and they said they did not wish to be any less faithful than the other towns, etc., and so they led us to another part of town a quarter of a league away, where there was a large cave containing many mummies; among these were three giants with deformed heads dressed in cumbi, though rotted with time. These are called the forebears of the townspeople, whom they worshiped and held in great esteem. There were also many traces of sacrifices, which we burned in the town along with the mummies. A great sorcerer, a descendant of these pagans, whom they say was a witch, had taken it upon himself to make sacrifices to them, and he had turned into an owl and had died eighteen years before. And he had left a command that since he had died in his paganism, and according to the law of his forefathers and kinsmen, he should be buried in a machay. And taking him out of the church they had done so. I sent my trusted Indian catechizer for this mummy, and it was brought to me along with the sacrifices made to it when they had gone to consult it after the man's death. We burned this mummy and those of the giants.

Beneath this huaca was another, in the midst of an enclosure, along with many bones of llamas (which are the sheep of this country) that had been sacrificed to him, along with trumpets and other instruments used in the sacrifices.

In the town of Quepas we dug up the real huaca Huamantucoc, for during the visit they had brought the visitor another in his place.

In the ruins of Cocha Líbiac, by digging down more than two yards, we came upon many traces of sacrifices and a store room made for the purpose. In it was the idol Mullu Cayan, sitting on a thin sheet of silver with many conopas around it. This small idol was made of bronze.

A stone's throw farther down we removed this huaca's brother, called Coto Tumac, which consisted of the pieces of the one Friar Francisco had burned. When this happened, the Indians say, there was much weeping and sorrow, and they sacrificed many llamas; the traces of this sacrifice are still visible.

I was greatly chagrined at first to see so little disposition toward piety on the part of the Indians and their church so poor that I mention it more in weeping than otherwise. But as Our Lord willed to move them by His word to reveal their beloved huacas, He moved them also to collect and to give a most liberal offering for an altar canopy, a backdrop, and a saint for the town, whose patron is Saint John the Baptist. I gave them the Charter of Servitude of Our Lady and taught them to say the rosary, and we returned with much joy to Huayllacayan, where I began as best I could to refute the errors listed on the register during the visit of Dr. Hernando de Avendaño. For the success of this undertaking we held our accustomed Christian teaching and rogation, and as a result the old men took us to the ruins of the town of Cotas, from which they had brought out the huaca Rimay during the visit, and they said that its father, Huaracáyac, had been burned by Friar Francisco. Our Lord did not will it to be hidden this time, and so, about an eighth of a league away from where its father was, with a little digging we came upon this idol and its many sacrifices. The pagan priest in charge of this huaca was sent into custody in Santa Cruz.

Another day we went to a place more than a league and a half away called Hunoyan. There were some chambers there built of carefully fitted stones, like the buildings in Cuzco, although more than half in ruins. From there Friar Francisco had taken out two famous and much-dreaded huacas to whom they sacrificed children, including some of tender age, because they said the huacas fed on human flesh. But after Friar Francisco had gone on his way, the Indians got together the pieces of their huacas and put them back in the place from which they now brought them out.

At a place called Chinchas, a league and a half from here, was the famous huaca of Usuy which, because of its great size, had escaped destruction during the visit. This time it did not do so, because I took with me many persons, unseated it from its foundations, broke it into many pieces, and burned the sacrifices along with the body of a great sorcerer whom they called the son of the huaca.

In the town of Chayna another huaca was undone. It could not be moved because it was huge, but we burned the sacrifices. They called this huaca Iusca, and we burned the three sons of this huaca, which were mummies.

The ruins of Ayáurac are about two and a half leagues from town on a road so bad and so rugged that one cannot get there on horseback. Despite this difficulty, we reached there and removed two huacas called husband and wife. The latter Friar Francisco had not discovered, and so, when he broke and burned the husband, the Indians put the pieces together again and worshiped them there. The buildings of this town seem to have been large and the Indians great idolaters. As such Our Lord has punished and destroyed them, for the only Indian left there was the priest of this huaca, and he is now in custody in Santa Cruz.

The huaca of the clan of Sopan, in his ancient town, was called Apu Xillin. Friar Francisco pulled this huaca down and burned it, but the Indians repaired it and kept it buried with many sacrifices and some silver. Dr. Hernando de Avendaño had already burned Huayna Xillin, the son of this one. I have followed in his footsteps and in those of the fathers of our Society in this preaching in order to claim success, for, to tell the truth, I thought that if I could not find a favorable disposition among these people, who had been warned that a visit was to come, and light for the errors known to exist among them, then I could profit but little by my eighteen years as a priest. Let us conclude with this town on the day of Our Lady's conception, which is that of Her vocation. Once again they enrolled themselves as the slaves of Our Lady, who has so greatly favored them. The movable huacas were sent to Lima, but the rest were burned, along with the mummies. The trumpets and eight and one-half marks of silver, which were found with the huacas, were also removed, and the ashes from the burning, which were found with the huacas, were thrown into the river so that they would not be able to put them together again.

All of the foregoing is from the aforementioned letter, from which it is plain that a second and third visit are needed. For proof of this, one might also mention the huacas that have been discovered by the priests with continual preaching since the visit. Dr. Pedro de Ortega, for instance, discovered many in Checras; Licentiate Francisco de Estrada found some in Mancas and Lampas; and Licentiate Miguel Rubio, a number in Huacho. From this the importance of continued preaching by the priests may be inferred. In the ensuing chapters we shall see some of the remedies for the extirpation of idolatry.

CHAPTER ELEVEN

The Means of Uprooting Idolatry

I SHOULD be very happy to hear a discussion of this point among experienced men who are zealous for the good of the Indian and to write down the means employed by others which have proved useful and efficacious. Meanwhile, I shall describe briefly the means that I know.

The two main causes of the idolatry of the Indians have already been given. The first is their vast ignorance of the matters of our faith, because they have not been taught to them, and the false conviction which they continue to hold concerning their huacas and superstitions, of which they have not been disillusioned. This too is for lack of Christian teaching and preaching, which must be strengthened not only by planting the truths of the Christian religion in their hearts, but also by uprooting the undergrowth and roots of their errors. The second reason is that up to now their huacas, malquis, conopas, and other incitements to idolatry have not been taken away. These two causes must be removed by missions, as I have said, and in the form of visits, as we shall now see. These missions must be conducted by intelligent persons, desirous of helping those whose need is great. The Indians must be taught slowly and confessed properly, as the circumstances require. As a result of the visit they should be deprived of their huacas and all that pertains to them in the manner that I shall describe concerning the procedures and instructions for a visit. But neither mission nor visit will be profitable, however long or permanent, if what is planted is not watered, cultivated, and nurtured, so that what has been pulled up by the roots may not spring up again. For however much has been done, much still remains, as we have seen.

When the mission in his town was ended a cacique had this to say:

"Father, things stand well now, but if I plow and dig and weed and water my garden once, and then don't see it or go near it for a year, what will it be like?"

And with this comparison he explained very well his idea with regard to the Christian teaching of the Indians. It is the continual care of the priest that counts. Therefore, His Illustrious Lordship has laid great stress by command and by very strict precepts to the priests to continue their work and not lift their hands from it, ordering them to teach Christian doctrine in person, to teach the catechism with particular care on Wednesdays and Fridays, and to preach every Sunday and on feast days. And in order to do their work with more zeal, and in order to show that they are doing it as they have been commanded to, let them write down their sermons and show them to the ordinary visitor of His Lordship. If anyone does not know how to do this, or is unable to do it, let him read the Indians a printed sermon at least on Sundays and feast days. No one can do less than this, and he has commanded specifically that a fine of ten pesos should be assessed upon the church immediately each time they fail to do so. The priest should be present in the towns of his mission according to the population, that is where there are fewer people a shorter time, where there are more people a longer time, etc.

Many priests are doing this, to the greater glory of Our Lord, the profit of the Indians, and their own happiness. One of them wrote me a letter a few days after he had reached his assigned mission, and I received it on the very day that this chapter was being printed. As a sample of many such I shall quote it. He writes:

I have read your message, over and over, Reverend Father, and it gives me courage not to falter on the road. For as God is my witness never have I worked so hard, nor with greater zeal and care. This mission was in a sad state and its people, unworthy of the name, seemed like beasts and savages, and lacking every good thing. There were more than a thousand confessed souls, but I could not find one of them who could recite the four prayers, except with a quantity of errors and misquotations. Some of the old men had gone for three years without hearing mass or having confessed, except to their huacas and heathen priests. What a pity! Except for the hasty and fleeting contact of these people with Sunday mass, and at festival time, and with the Wednesday and Friday teaching it seems as if they have had no priest. This has broken my heart and I have often wept with them, telling them their many faults: how they were without Christian teaching, without God, and without law. They shrug their shoulders and say "Checan, checan, Señor Padre," (that is the truth, that is the truth) kissing my clothing and my feet in admiration. Every day for four months, for two hours in the morning and two hours in the afternoon, without missing a single day, I personally have gotten together in the cemetery all the boys and girls, and the old men and women, of whom there are more than two hundred. There I have taught them, catechized them, and indoctrinated them in the principles of our holy faith, and then in the four prayers, the confession, the articles, and the catechism. And now no one is ignorant of these things. I experience a thousand glories and a feeling of contentment to see them pray and hear them sing the hymns and songs I have taught them. I thank God for His infinite grace that by His blessed blood He grieves for them and for me. Certainly I need it badly, as I lack (and I confess it at times) the patience to know when to use love and a reward, and when harshness and punishment, telling them that I will have to send them to the house in Santa Cruz. They are afraid of that, and so they come together to mass and to Christian teaching. This house is their bogey, their punishment, their prison, their whip, and I think it the greatest thing, the most saintly, the best, and most pious thing that has been done.

Thus far the priest's letter.

His Excellency also contributes for his part to the same end. He has ordered that any town that is being lived in again without governmental order, after it has been abandoned for a consolidated town, may be burned by the visitor and so demolished that the Indians will return to the consolidated towns.[a] This has been done in many cases, but if in the opinion of the visitor some that remain separate should be consolidated, he should so inform His Excellency so that their reduction may be ordered. These measures, if carried out, will be efficacious and the Indians will receive the Christian teaching that they need. But what most requires efficiency is the punctual execution of His Lordship's orders, so that all priests who are candidates for a mission station, or such religious as present themselves for consideration, shall, in addition to the usual test of their knowledge of the Indian language, be required to preach in it publicly. And they should be given suggested topics for a sermon on the previous day. And all who were already in charge of missions when this edict was promulgated should present themselves within eight months to His Lordship to preach in public like the rest. For it is obvious that anyone who is ready and willing to preach will do so if he desires, and in order that he may so desire he will be given the opportunity, but anyone who does not know how to preach cannot do so, however often he is ordered to do so.

His Lordship's command has greatly encouraged those who know the language well, because they realize that they will be able to pass the test and make a demonstration of their skill. Those who do not know the language will work hard to learn it in order not to be deprived of their missions. Those who do not know it and are good linguists hope that since they have a talent for it they will find an opportunity to use it.

[a] For greater ease in collecting taxes and generally controlling the Indian population, the government ordered certain towns abandoned and told their inhabitants to go and live in a consolidated town. Frequently, as can be inferred from this passage, the Indians disobeyed, returning to their former villages, to which they were understandably much attached.

For if in a contest between missions, and on other occasions of honor and profit, the prelates take the trouble to remember the absent and to better the station of or to promote those who have lived up to their obligations in the missions which they have served by assigning them to better churches and missions and by giving them less work and greater advantages, the priests would all be encouraged to do their job better. As the proverb says, *Addere calcaria sponte currenti.*

In this matter of the preaching by the priests, as in other matters for the good of the Indians, everything is well ordered and provided for by the decrees of the Synod issued five years ago, and there is no reason to expect or require anything more than their proper execution. These decrees command the priests to be careful and diligent in confessing the Indians, in catechizing them, and in preparing them for Communion. After Easter each priest should send parish lists of their missions to His Illustrious Lordship so that he, having seen them, may order those who have confessed to be marked with a C, and with two C's those who have taken Communion. I have brought some of these lists given me by the priests to His Illustrious Lordship. On a Quasimodo Sunday, as I was going through a town, I served Communion to more than a hundred Indians whom their priest had prepared for it, and both on the preceding day and that same morning they all came back to confession. In another town a like number had already taken Communion on Easter. The place had been visited the year before as I, since I was present, can testify. Of all the towns previously visited, whether large or small, none had less idolatry than this one, a seeming verification of a remark by the supreme pontiff, Clement VIII, of happy memory: *Non erunt vere Christiani donec communicent in Paschate.*

By such efficacious means is the Devil variously foiled and turned away. A Dominican father, a man of credit and authority, assured me that once, when he had warned the Indians of a town under his jurisdiction to come to Communion on Easter if they were prepared for it, the Devil raised such a noise and confusion that night that the surrounding hills seemed to be falling down. The Devil even appeared to the Indians visibly, saying the town would be destroyed if they took Communion. They all went in terror to the fathers, therefore, not knowing the cause of the racket and noise that they had heard. The latter quieted the Indians, and with the dawn of a clear, serene day they were finally enlightened.

The lack of ornament in the churches comes more from a lack of interest on the part of certain priests than from lack of money, for in addition to what is derived from each year's compulsory contribution to the church, even though such funds are under the control of the *corregidor*, His Excellency orders a special contribution to be made whenever he is informed of the need. And it would be helpful for the visitor to be given similar instructions. The Indians contribute readily to such expenditures either by providing farms for the purpose or in other ways, if encouraged to do so. In one town, in a single evening, the Indians got together more than three hundred and fifty pesos to buy a pennant, a silver cross, a feretory,[b] a statue of the infant Jesus, and other things necessary for the brotherhood which had been set up for them.

I must point out that we must be careful of the kind of sacristans that are hired, for I know one case where the individual drank the wine that was provided for the mass; to keep from being found out he added a corresponding amount of water.

Two aspects of the Holy Sacrament of the Altar, that is, the adornment of the church and the divine worship itself, as proper and necessary for Christianity, were greatly encouraged by the Lord Bishop of Cuzco Don Fernando de Mendoza, whose fame will live long in this kingdom. It was he who first commanded sternly that all the priests of his bishopric should instruct their parishioners and prepare them to take Communion at least on Easter and not deny them the viaticum when ill. And he had them establish ciboria, monstrances,

[b] Portable platform on which statues are carried in religious processions. *Infra*, p. 132, n. *d*.

and repositories in the churches of each town so that whenever a priest was present he would have the Blessed Sacrament. Sometimes he did this at his own expense and at other times he helped with large donations. In a town that I know of, the priest was condemned in a case involving a large sum of money, and the archbishop told him the condemnation was well deserved and that he should have a ciborium made with his name and coat of arms upon it as if he were making a gift, and this was done. It is very common for a single priest to be in charge of four or five towns, and it is not right for the Blessed Sacrament to be available for a viaticum only in the town where the priest is. Therefore, to prevent the sick of the other towns from dying without it, he called a meeting of the serious men of all orders. And overcoming many objections, he had a number of reliquaries made so that any time the priest was called upon, he might carry the Blessed Sacrament to another town, bearing it in a reliquary hanging about his neck in a little velvet case on a silken cord of very curious gold. This will seem new and strange to anyone but little acquainted with church history and who has not observed what happens elsewhere. I was once about to pass through the gate of a fairly small walled town in Italy, called Monte Falco, where they have the miraculous body of Santa Clara, which took the name of the town, when I saw a priest come out carrying the Blessed Sacrament from the town to a house in the country. He was accompanied to the city gate by many persons who came to receive his benediction. Then he went alone on his way, accompanied by the sacristan, who carried a lighted lantern.

As for the second point, the adornment of the churches, the bishop had brought from Spain, where he was consecrated, many beautiful ornaments. When he came to his bishopric he divided them all among the towns that he passed through, and when he reached Cuzco he had but a single ornament left. He had ordered from Spain about a thousand yards of damask and velvet for hanging in his house, but perceiving the lack of ornament in the Indian churches, he ordered the goods all used to decorate them. Thus he never had in his own house anything but a small backdrop for his chapter room. The affairs of this great prelate cannot be told so quickly, however, but would require a longer and better story. In this connection much more could also be said about the lord archbishop of this city (who is in glory), Don Toribio Alphonso Mogrovejo. It once fell to his lot to consecrate the altar stone in a certain town, and he was so long gone that when he returned he had nothing left of his pontifical goods, having given them all away as alms. In Moyobamba, because there was no cross to be used in processions, he left the cross of his own standard. This they still have and esteem it as they should.

Many priests are diligent in this, for they can see its value with their own eyes. This week a most conscientious priest wrote me as follows:

I certify to you, Reverend Father, that one works both spiritually and corporally, since my desire is simply for them to know the mercy which Our Lord uses with them daily to soften their hearts, which are hard toward the good, and to this end I labor as His Majesty knows. I have to give an account of each soul, and to the extent that I am able to I do so. I would be pleased, Reverend Father, if you could come and see the fruit of my labors and the devotion they show in attending the Divine Sacraments and in everything else, and even in the ornamentation of the church, which, since I have been here, I have been urging them to do. They come with good will and bring alms which are generous for Indians, because in every town I have created luxurious Communion vessels, and in them I place the Blessed Sacrament when I visit them. They come to look at them with great devotion, and I feel endless contentment as I watch them, and wish they were all saints, and so forth.

The only remedy for the evil caste of teachers and ministers of idolatry, or at the least to effect a reduction in their numbers, is to send them into custody in Santa Cruz, which frightens them. More than fourteen hundred pesos have been spent for this up to now, because the Lord Viceroy, Prince of

Esquilache, told me to establish this work energetically. It would be useful to have a place like it in each bishopric, and with a little good fortune it would be easy to support one. Where there is no house to confine them in, we could divide them among the monasteries, hospitals, and other establishments of pious folk to be kept, taught, and supported. To allow these old people to remain in their villages is wrong and is a leading cause of their misbelief, but since we cannot remove them all, as they are numerous, the principal one in each town should be sent, and this will frighten the rest. It is well for them to be pointed out and known, so that they can be made to come to Christian instruction with the children and sit with them in church. Thus they will come to be held in low esteem in the town. It is important above all for those who backslide to be severely punished. On the other hand, as most of them are old and poor and only exercise their profession in order to eat, they ought to be helped with alms, thus encouraging among the Indians the practice of this virtue of which they have so little knowledge and experience. I once saw the people of a town encouraged in this by their priest. He stood at the door of the church as they came out of mass and begged alms for the poor. He did not want silver but things in kind, such as corn, potatoes, peppers, eggs, and the like, and he made a great pile of these things and then divided them among the poor. As his own share, this priest bought a half a measure of corn, some potatoes and meat, and for our part we bought an equal amount. It is barely to be believed how much good could be done if matters were so organized, which would not be hard to do. All the priests I have told about this have tried it out with great consolation to themselves and no less pleasure and profit to the Indians.

Corporal nourishment is least important of all unless the Indians are deprived thereby of the opportunity for idolatry and superstition. They learn Christian charity and piety both by giving and by receiving, and their good will is thereby increased, so that they can better accept what they are told and what they are taught. For this reason we made a practice in every town of visiting the sick and taking them some raisins or a little bread or something of the kind, and however little they receive they are grateful. Usually when we enter a town for the first time the children run away from us, but after I gave them a dozen figs or a handful of raisins one day, not a one of them now stays away from us. And their mothers and fathers follow them.

Many of the sorcerers are *ambicamayos*, as they call themselves, or healers, but they precede their cures with superstitious and idolatrous practices. The priests should examine and instruct those who are to perform healing in order to get rid of what is superstitious and evil therein, and to profit by what is good, for example, their knowledge and use of certain herbs and other simples used in their treatments.

The only way to make the curacas and caciques behave (and the fact that they do not is, as I have said, an important cause of idolatry) is to begin at the beginning and instruct their children so that from childhood they may learn the Christian discipline and doctrine. Their fathers are grateful for this, and one cacique, after sending his elder son to boarding school, told me that he wanted to send two others, and that if His Lordship could not maintain them all, he himself would pay for their upkeep. And he asked how much money he would have to pay each year.

By His Majesty's order, another boarding school is to be founded in Cuzco and one in Charcas,° which are the three chief places in this kingdom. The number of students will not be limited. All the sons of the caciques and second persons, as they call them, of every town may attend. They will be well fed and given the necessary clothing by the fathers of our Society, according to our statutes regarding the care and education of youth. Provisions have already been sent from this city, as I shall presently relate, for the boarding schools of Cuzco and Charcas.

While they are still profiting by these schools, where they

° La Plata. The third place, by inference, is Lima.

will spend some years, it is most important during missions and visits to gain the confidence of the caciques by treating them well and honoring them, neither asking anything of them nor taking anything from them (though some of them want to give small presents of things to eat and are upset if they are not accepted), giving them such devotional materials as we have with us. Because, when we have won over the curacas, there is no difficulty about discovering the huacas and idolatrous practices. They must be used to this end, and those who are stubborn and rebellious, as some are, should have all the rigor of the law applied to them. Upon them must be executed what the Lord Archbishop ordered in his edict of last August 30, and His Excellency in his decree of last September 10, to wit, that curacas and caciques who, within two days of the reading of the edict, shall not have pointed out and made manifest the idolatry of their town, declaring whether they are teachers thereof, shall be deprived of their office, whipped, shorn, and brought to the house of Santa Cruz.

If they are accomplices of idolatry, they shall be deprived of their position as cacique, reduced to forced labor, whipped, and shorn. And if idolatry exists in the town or festivals, and superstition, intoxication, or habitual drunkenness, and they say that they do not know about these things (for if they do exist it is virtually impossible for the curacas and caciques not to know it), they will be deprived of their office and sentenced to forced labor. These decrees are read and explained at the beginning of the visit, and if they carry out their provisions as therein prescribed, this alone will be sufficient to rid the kingdom of idolatry.

In order to uproot and get rid of drunkenness, a very ancient root of idolatry, His Excellency and His Illustrious Lordship, each to the extent that it concerns him, has set forth many remedies, ordering the priests not to sell wine to the Indians under pain of excommunication and a fine of 20 valid pesos. For the *corregidors* the penalty is a sum equal to twice the value of what has been sold. In conformity with the orders of Don Francisco de Toledo, His Excellency has commanded that an Indian who gets drunk, even if he is the leading cacique, should be admonished and warned not to repeat his offense. The second time he should be exiled for two months, and the third time he becomes ineligible to be a cacique or to hold public office. The fourth time he should be exiled from the region for six months and lose the salary of his office. If he perseveres in his vice, he shall be exiled forever and His Excellency shall give his post to someone else. If the offender is a common Indian, he shall be reprimanded the first time, given twenty lashes the second time, and the town crier shall announce why he got drunk. The third time he shall be shorn and the fourth time exiled and subjected to the remaining penalties in force. All this has been very well ordered and agreed upon and if it were carried out, drunkenness among the Indians would soon disappear. But who will carry it out?

The matter of dissimulating with the Indians and punishing them is worthy of attention and remedy, for there is a common opinion among the priests that they do not dare to lay their hands upon an Indian but must let them do as they like. For on the slightest provocation, four or five Indians conspire together to bear false witness and accuse their priest. And it has often been said to me that it would be more advantageous to let some deeds remain unpunished and totally unremedied than to accept the testimony of Indians against priests, since the former see no harm in swearing falsely. But if they are convicted of this crime, they should be severely punished.

In the same decrees of His Excellency and of His Illustrious Lordship, the punishment is indicated for those who relapse into idolatry. And the day that punishment is enforced there will be improvement. No one is punished for a first offense. All are pardoned, and during the visit they are solemnly absolved at the church door. Thus they acquire a great notion of that outward ceremony. A Spaniard told me of having met some Indians going rapidly along the road. He asked them where they were going and they replied: we are going to become good Christians, striking ourselves with staves at the church door, thus explaining in their own words their idea of solemn absolution.

For the same purpose it is important to carry out His Lordship's orders, and the ordinary visitor, after he has read the regular edict of the visit, should also read the edict that is usually read concerning idolatry, the decrees of His Excellency, and the edicts of the Lord Archbishop against it and against drunkenness. In the towns already visited, let them inquire diligently whether there has been backsliding and let them punish it. And this advantage among others, and a not insignificant one, will follow if the Indians know they are going to be visited every year: that they will realize that the visitor does not come merely to see their priest, and they will refrain from being insolent to him and from criticizing him with or without reason. It would also be most useful for the visitor to know the Indian language and to speak it properly.

But the first, handiest, and most efficacious remedy, which will encompass all the rest, is the first visit, already mentioned. How this is to be done I will explain in the following chapters.

CHAPTER TWELVE

What Sort of Visitor Is Needed for
the Extirpation of Idolatry

IN THE GATHERING already referred to, which was called together by the Lord Viceroy Prince of Esquilache, and at which were present gentlemen of the Royal Audience, members of the Ecclesiastical Chapter, and serious and experienced men of religion, the most important point that was decided was to build a house of detention for sorcerers in the town of the Cercado outside the walls of this city. I was ordered to draw up a plan, to begin properly, and to devote all my energies to the building so that the project might be well started before I set out on the mission. As soon as the house was ready, and even before, the most guilty sorcerers of the towns being visited were being sent there.

The second decision made during the consultation was that a boarding school should be founded for the caciques, and therefore our house in the Cercado, which had previously been used for the novitiate, was adapted to this purpose. After the Lord Viceroy had written his New Year's letter to the caciques, fourteen of their sons came together from the various provinces. His Excellency ordered them to be furnished green shirts and trousers and a red striped cape. This, together with everything else that was needful—shoes, stockings, and hat—was to be the uniform of the school boys. His Excellency came with the city officials to our house to attend mass on New Year's Day. Before it began, His Excellency placed on each with his own hand a band of crimson taffeta which crossed the right shoulder and went beneath the left arm, with a little silver shield bearing the royal arms upon the breast. The advantage of these two policies, which are to be continuous and unchanging, will not be seen as quickly as the results of the third, that is to send suitable visitors to uncover a deeply rooted, well hidden, and all-but-invisible evil. For the Indians have been performing their ceremonies and pagan sacrifices in the sight of all, yet they have not been recognized as such. The task was to enlighten those who were deceived, to teach those to whom little or nothing had been taught, to give them a general pardon, to treat them with mercy, and to proceed with some slight rigor of justice against the rebellious and stubborn. For this purpose, visitors were chosen who were experienced in Indian affairs, who knew the language, and who had some skill in the pulpit. They had also be be learned men and theologians who knew how to make themselves understood and how to teach ignorant people the mysteries of our holy faith. They had to undo and refute errors consonant with their ability, errors never previously corrected, to which they were born and in which, until now, they have lived.

Above all else, if the visitors are given suitable backing, they should make known by word and deed that the visit attempts nothing but the glory of God and well-being of souls, *et quaerunt, non quae sua sunt, sed quae Iesu Christi,* taking literally what was said in another context: *da mihi animas, caetera tolle tibi.* They should not treat the Indians in any way that smacks of self-interest, but let it appear that what they do is done with great joy, taking nothing from them but giving liberally to them. They must not let their servants or officials who accompany them be the slightest burden to the Indians nor hurt them in any way, and if they do so they should punish them as an example. A visitor would, therefore, seem to have acted properly if on arriving in a town he ordered a proclamation read saying that no Indian should give anything to his servants even if they asked for it, and that he would punish anyone found guilty of such conduct.

If the visitor desires to be, as I say, less of a burden and more of a profit to the Indians, he should take with him the least possible baggage and the fewest possible servants, despite the fact that the roads are proverbially difficult and dangerous. A notary should go along, as he will be frequently needed, even though the visitor does most of his own writing. Nor can one do without a crown agent, who is indispensable. But the latter should not be an Indian, for I have known this to cause serious complications. He should rather be a diligent and trustworthy person.

Nor, despite attempted urbanities and courtesies, should the visitor permit the Spaniards, of whom there are always some among the Indians, to accompany him or the religious. Most important, and a *sine qua non*, the visitor must be accompanied by monks to preach, to catechize, and confess the Indians. For a visit has more to do with the heart than with the body, and more relation to industry than to force, and pertains more to mercy than to justice. Indeed, the paraphernalia and tumult of justice must be curtailed as much as can be, and Christian teaching, sermons, and confessions emphasized, so that the visitor, like the fathers who go with him, may show that he and they are in effect fathers and teachers and not crown agents or judges.

Some of the members of our Society have had doubts about the way visits have been carried out and practiced up to now, and they deem it improper for the fathers to go with the visitors at all. They say that the Indians, although they are timid and cowardly, will not fear the fathers so much as they fear the visitor and will retract their confessions to us or confess badly. Therefore, it would be better for the visitor to go alone, doing his duty, discovering and removing huacas, and that the religious could then come afterward and do their work without the visitor's having to depend on the fathers or the fathers on the visitor.

Experience affords a sufficient reply, for this has been tried. The fathers have sometimes gone to Indian towns without a visitor and they have not been successful in gathering the people together for a single sermon, let alone for many. The fact is that more are needed to teach them patiently than are needful to make them confess, as necessity requires this first time. Although it is true that once a town has been visited, the Indians are so affectionate and so well pleased with the benefits they have received, that when the fathers return to their towns they greet them with extraordinary signs of joy, and when they are about to leave they bid them farewell with no less grief and feeling. On our return from a visit, six of us reached a town together, and the Indians would not let us move on for two days, keeping us busy because of their piety hearing confessions from morning to night. This was during an off-season festival, whereas previously, during Lent, which it was their obligation to observe, they had shown no little reluctance.

It is possible for the fathers to succeed in discovering huacas through the force of their preaching, but this has happened but rarely. Many missions have been undertaken by the fathers alone, without a visitor, in some of the towns already visited, but in towns not yet visited, where huacas are to be uncovered, it is unwise for the fathers to go alone.

For their part, the visitors do not like to go without the fathers, for aside from the fact that their presence carries much authority among both Indians and Spaniards, they need them for counsel when they find themselves perplexed or in doubt. By the presence of the fathers the visitors can defend themselves from the slanders that are frequently put upon them. Of this we could adduce many examples. And since the purpose of a visit is to discover idolatry and remove huacas, the greatest assistance comes from the fathers, who talk to the Indians frequently, relieve their fears, and move among them with their sermons. For the Indians come to them as if to fathers who love them well and intercede for them with the visitor. And the main task, that of teaching, although the visitor often preaches, is the work of the fathers and is carried on through the usual catechisms and sermons. As for confession, this is a matter for the fathers only, and we have explained to the Indians the difference between the confession and the examination that takes place in the visitor's presence. And we have not experienced (*quantum humana fragilitas nosse potest*) rebellion, difficulty, or deceit in the confession. On the contrary, things hidden during the visitor's examination concerning idolatry have been revealed therein.

Thus, as experience has shown, neither the fathers alone nor the visitor alone can fulfill the intended purpose, that is, to make the Indians reveal and give up their huacas, malquis, and conopas and the like, to convince them of their errors, instruct them in the mysteries of our faith, and absolve them through the confession of the sins in which they have lived all their lives. This is our purpose, and visitors and fathers are like two partial causes which bring about the same effect.

CHAPTER THIRTEEN

What a Visitor Should Do upon Reaching a Town, Distribution of Time and Sermons

THE FIRST day is the most difficult and arduous, as all beginnings are. It is even more difficult in this enterprise where a new start is being made. Therefore one must proceed with patience and prayer.

For this reason, a visit is not begun in a large town nor in the capital of a province, but in some remote and faraway place, in a small town. If this town is near one that has already been visited, and if by this means or some other a glimpse of the idolatry in the town has been obtained, we will have gained a great deal. Therefore let it be spoken of. Let the priest and caciques of the town be forewarned in time where they are to go and of the day the visitor is to arrive so that the people may be assembled to receive him, as indicated above. When he is received in church, one of the fathers should make a short talk to relieve the people of their fears, explaining that the purpose of the visit is not to punish but to teach. He will also tell them at this time that they are to come together every day early in the morning for the sermon, that in the afternoon the bell will ring for catechism and that none must be absent, as they are to be called according to the poll list.

It is especially important to forewarn the *camachicos*[a] of the clans and the alcaldes and crown agents about this so that they can call the people together, making a special effort to win over the most important people, for when they have been won over there will be no difficulty with the rest.

Inquiry then is made about the sick of the town and a father goes to visit them, taking them some little thing

---

[a] *Camachico* or *kamachikuq*. One who rules; ruler of the clan.

brought for the purpose. As he goes along the road, it is also well to be provided with some pieces of bread, or something of the sort, to give to the Indians whom he meets.

The hours of the day are to be divided as follows: at sunup, or just before, mass is said. During the first or second mass, the bell is rung to call the people together to hear the second or third mass, which is the one they always attend. During the masses they are commended to Our Lord, asking Him to enlighten them and soften their hearts. When mass is over, a father gives them their Christian teaching. After this there is a sermon which does not last longer than a half an hour, or at the most three-quarters, so that by eight o'clock mass, teaching and sermon are over.

If there is time and it seems appropriate, the people can be assembled more easily by going out in a procession, carrying a standard, ringing a bell, and singing the Christian doctrine with the first four or five persons who appear, even though the four prayers have not yet been sung when the whole town is assembled.

After the sermon, those who are to be examined by the visitor or questioned by the fathers as to Christian doctrine should remain. All this must be done during the first days, for thereafter confession and teaching will last until about noon, which is the time for eating. At about two-thirty the bell rings again, and not everyone comes, but only that clan which has been sent for to be questioned, catechized, and confessed. This exercise lasts until about sunset. About half an hour before this, the bell rings for the Indians to come to catechism, which is taught to them properly by parts.

On Sunday mass is later because people generally come in from other towns. Catechism is taught in the afternoon, rosaries and images are distributed among them, with which it is well to be provided, as prizes. After this there is usually a procession, and on this occasion as on others some songs are sung to them in their language, which pleases the Indians greatly. They sing them and repeat them, and, because it is appropriate for them to know them, printed copies are distrib-

uted. Since sermons have to be in good order if they are to
be delivered properly, a learned man who is a good linguist
should prepare them. They should also be printed, which I
devoutly hope will be done for the aid and profit of all.

The sermons should be appropriate to their capacity, arguing
with them and convincing them by natural reasons that they
can understand, rather than by samples of fine writing. I
noticed that one of the visitors did this very well. To refute
their error concerning their pacarinas and the belief that some
persons have their origin in a certain hill, and others in a
certain fountain, he taught them, with many reasonings, that
like produces like. To refute another error, that is, the belief
that all men do not come from our first fathers, in the midst
of the catechism he brought out an ear of corn, asking them
how many kernels it took to produce it, answering that it
came from a single one. Well then, he asked, as this kernel
is white or red, or has but one color only, do some kernels
come out white, others black, and others gray? To show them
that they should not worship the lightning, he taught in a way
that they could understand how the lightning bolts are made,
how the clouds freeze, etc. They say that he even convinced
one of the Incas that the sun could not be a god merely by
reasoning that it could not stop its motion when and as it
wished. The pleasure with which they receive these things is
incredible. And how well this demonstrates how natural it
is for man to understand and to know. This is the way sermons
ought to be:

First, it must always show that there is not and cannot be
more than one God, and that huacas are not and cannot be God.

Second, that God is the creator of all things, that He created
the world and the angels; it should treat of the fall, and how
the demons, in order to hurt man and avenge themselves
upon God, invented huacas and other superstitions.

Third, about the creation of our first parents, and how we
are all descended from them, refuting the error they have that
each clan has its separate origin and pacarina.

Fourth, how the Devil deceived our first parents about

original sin, and how from it arise all the sins and errors of the world.

Fifth, of the coming of Christ, Our Lord, to heal man, lifting him out of sin and teaching the road to Heaven, and how He sent his apostles to preach, and founded His church.

Sixth, of the laws that He left to His church that it should keep His commandments, and of the five laws of the church.

Seventh, that as a remedy for sin He left the sacraments, explaining to them especially the hour of Penance and all that goes with it, as is proper. This sermon is always preached when they are about to confess in order to teach them that the sorcerers to whom they confess do not have the power to forgive sins.

Eighth, of the intercession of the saints and the adoration of images, for they say that these are huacas, and in this as in other things they are quite ignorant. As it happened, there were four images of saints, and very good ones, in a certain town, representing the vocation of the four brotherhoods. And it was discovered that the Indians did not commend themselves to these saints nor say prayers to them because they said those saints were already theirs. They had bought them, and so for this reason they went to other towns to visit other saints.

Ninth, how to commend themselves to the Lord Our God and to the Blessed Virgin. In particular, they must be taught how to say the rosary and how to pray to their guardian angel when they go to bed and when they arise, etc.

Tenth, this has to do with the festival of the cross, of its virtues, which the Devil fears, of holy water, and how to use it in their infirmities and trials.

Eleventh, concerning the mass and the Blessed Sacrament of the Altar, and how they are to prepare themselves to receive it.

Twelfth, concerning the judgment, punishment, and eternal glory.

All these matters are also treated in the catechism by putting questions to them, having them answer, and trying to have them achieve some idea of what is being taught.

When one expects to be in a town for a longer period, either because the town is large or otherwise, these materials can be stretched out a bit. When one is there for a briefer time two sermons are combined, for opposite reasons.

Wednesdays and Fridays there is Penance and when they come for this purpose they bring with them sticks which they have made and say that since they are punished on their backs any sort will do. On these days, when the catechism is over at nightfall, they are told a parable, and all the women go home. The men remain to do Penance, and are sung to, or the Miserere is recited to them, with interruptions for acts of contrition.

They should be exhorted during catechism to own images of saints and to bring rosaries with them. Many are distributed among them as prizes for knowing the doctrine. They are also taught to make them out of the large *chaquira* beads,[b] which their wives wear as ornaments around their necks. Or they can make them of cords with knots, like *quipus*,[c] although most of them send for them and buy them whenever they can. A Spaniard told me he needed no better profit than to follow the fathers, selling rosaries to the Indians. In many towns few Indians had rosaries when we arrived, and when we left there were few who did not. To teach them to pray the rosary, we pray aloud with them sometimes.

We not only teach them the catechism and Christian doctrine but, during the first days, as I have remarked, while the visitor is busy finding out about and locating huacas, we gather a number of them together and examine each one separately, in the hearing of the rest. We see whether he knows at least the Pater Noster, the Credo, and the essential points of the catechism. We begin with the younger, unmarried men and women, who generally know the most, and tell them to teach

[b] Colored glass beads of Peru.
[c] Knotted cords, used by the Incas as a mnemonic device.

their parents at home. In this examination we are aided by the crown agents and by blind Indians and others who know the doctrine well. During this last mission a lame Indian went with us to every town. He is now with Licentiate Rodrigo Hernández. Of him I have already said that he knew his doctrine well, having learned it in our house. To those who were examined and approved, a piece of paper was given admitting them to confession. Afterward it seemed better and more practical to give them a small piece of crude silver, or a bit of worked silver as a token. There are many of these to be found among the ornaments of a huaca. One can also use for this purpose chaquira beads of a certain color and of a variety which the Indians do not possess, to keep them from deceiving the confessor.

Confessions must begin after the visitor has inquired about the huacas and idolatrous practices of individuals and has solemnly absolved them for their failure to take Communion. He begins with the unmarried men and women, although ordinarily and more properly he does so after they have revealed to him their huacas, conopas, and other instruments of idolatry.

When they go to confession, they give the confessor the token to show that they know the doctrine, and no one is admitted to confession without it. After confession, he gives them another token so that they may be written down as having confessed. But the surest way is for each confessor to write down the names of those he has heard in confession, for in this way there can be no cheating, since by tokens alone we have sometimes been deceived. The people must generally be confessed by careful questioning and examination, refusing to accept the little that they talk about and much less so the statements of the old men, who are very weak in memory. When we speak of confession, we should tell them to make quipus to confess by, for many Indians use them well for this purpose. In the sermon or catechism we can help them understand the *Jubileo* which His Holiness Pope Paul V gave us for people in missions everywhere. It must be explained to them in terms suitable to their capacity what the *Jubileo* is so that they may desire to win it. They must be taught what plenary indulgence is and how helpful it would be to win that also. It is fitting to give them only light penance so that they may perform it immediately, I approved the action of some of the fathers who gave their own rosary to the penitent who was on his knees praying the whole time that he was confessing the next one, and thus the rosary passed from one to another.

CHAPTER FOURTEEN

How a Visit Should Be Begun

THE DAY AFTER one's arrival all the townspeople should be received according to the poll list, if this has not already been done the day before, to see whether the missing persons are readily able to come.

When the people are gathered together, mass is sung, said, or prayed, and at the end of the doctrine, at the time of the sermon, the edict is read to them. It is taught and explained in their language; then the first sermon is preached, exhorting them in this, as in everything else, to reveal their huacas and idolatry and to show them to the visitor without fear.

On the second day, His Excellency's decrees against drunkenness and idolatry, which were printed last year, are read and the matter of pardons for those who denounce others will be carefully explained, as well as the penalties for those who do not.

It must be assumed that there can be no time limit set for a visit in a given town beyond the requirements of the situation. It would be a mistake to move on simply because nothing is found out immediately after arrival, for in this way all the expected results will be lost. It has sometimes happened that at the start of a visit, even after several days, nothing has been discovered. Then with diligence and industry, with continual sermons and catechisms, with patience and long-suffering born of prayer, Our Lord has moved the Indians to make revelations. To this end it is most effective throughout the visit to repeat the litany daily after mass, while the people are still assembled. The important thing is thus to acquire an entering wedge by hearing about some one huaca in a town, or about the sorcerer who guards it. The Indians freely offer information about neighboring towns and will then give themselves away easily. The beginning is the hardest and one has to win by one means or another, as experience will demonstrate.

Our first goal is to win over some reasonable Indian by offering him rewards in secret and by telling him that no other living person will find out what he has said. He should be persuaded to tell about the town's most important huaca and about the sorcerer who guards it, and everything else that he knows about it. On this first occasion no more should be expected, but one should thank the Indian and pay him for the little that he has revealed.

The second move is to summon to the visitor's house some apparently intelligent old Indian, keeping him away from his comrades so that he can talk to the visitor and the fathers privately. They should give him presents and be kind to him and say they have not come to punish him or the rest of the Indians, but to make them good Christians and to lead them out of the blindness in which the Devil keeps them; that the remedy is for him to make known and tell about the huacas of his town; that he should not be afraid, etc. If he says that he has no information, tell him to think carefully but do not insist this first time. Be kind to him, give him something to eat, and then come back to the subject a few hours later, or the next day, urging him with more insistence. If he still says he knows nothing, tell him the Devil is hardening his heart to keep him from confessing his sins and to prevent him from going to Heaven, etc. This reasoning, which admits of no reply, will convince him. In the time of the Inca all the Indians worshiped huacas because they knew no other god. They said the huaca was their creator and by worshiping it they would have more cattle and corn and would live longer. Some of the huacas are hills and high places which time cannot consume. Therefore, supposing the Indian could have known the Inca, or was born but a little time after the Spaniards arrived, he must surely know the huacas that his father worshiped and left to him when he died. For up to now no secular or ecclesiastical judicial action had deprived them of the huacas that they had in the days of the Inca. For this reason, he must give an accounting thereof or be punished for refusing to talk, as the princes have commanded. You must insist several times in this way, asking again and again, arguing with him, and letting the visitor talk to him, for he will be more determined to make him speak; then his priest and after him the fathers should question him.

The third measure is to summon the cacique privately and at an unseasonable hour so that no one can see him come. Tell him that if he does not reveal the huacas and sorcerers of his town he will be exiled and deprived of his office. And one should reiterate the decrees previously mentioned. To convince him, repeat the second reason, which is the more powerful.

Fourth. Ask the cacique, or some other reasonable Indian, where the pacarina from which he descends is located, for it is customary for the Indians to worship their pacarina. Ask him in friendly conversation about other ancient matters, such as where the old men say the souls went before the Spaniards told them about Heaven and Hell. The cacique certainly knows all about the huacas and their fables and antiquities. When this has been accomplished, ask about the huacas of neighboring towns, thus acquiring information about them and their priests and ministers, which is very important.

Fifth. Ask who are the healers of the town and, as you fetch them, take them aside to talk about healing. Examine them very secretly, for it is very common for healers to be also ministers of idolatry.

Remember to keep these Indians in a secret place so that

they cannot communicate with each other even if, after several days, they have not yet told anything. Keep on talking to them, convincing them with reasons, among which should be the statement that the huacas of all the neighboring towns have been discovered. After a few attempts, the thread will surely be discovered and after it the bobbin. Let them be warned also that in an inquiry into idolatry they cannot keep the least bit back, for nothing will be done but to find out the truth, accommodating it to the order of justice.

Sixth. As a clue to the identity of sorcerers, it may be foreseen that they are either old men and women or persons crippled, lame, or one-eyed, or peculiar in some other way, as we have noted and as experience has shown. There are, however, Indian boys who have inherited the office from their parents.

Seventh. When it has been discovered or demonstrated that one of those interrogated has continued to hide his huacas or his identity as a sorcerer, he must be punished publicly, although moderately in a manner more calculated to seem insulting than to seem severe. To shear them upsets them greatly, as the queue is regarded as an important ornament. For this ceremony the whole town should be called together, and a proclamation should declare that the individual is not being punished because he owned huacas or was a sorcerer, but because he refused to reveal himself and lied when asked about it.

CHAPTER FIFTEEN

How a Sorcerer or Any Other Indian Who Reveals or Gives Information about Huacas Is to Be Examined

WHAT HAS been said in the previous chapter serves but to call attention to the quarry, so to speak. Let us now see how we are to hunt it down and how we are to examine the sorcerer or other person giving the information.

In the first place, the examination must be performed by the visitor alone, without a notary or any other person present, because of the fear of the Indians and their reticence about revealing a secret so many years hidden. They are convinced that whoever hears them speak will give them away and accuse them to the rest of the town. They are especially inclined to refuse to talk about the huacas of a clan or faction other than their own lest, when it is known, they be faced with it and others should accuse them of having denounced them. The examination is to be conducted by the use of the following questions, with the warning to the Indians that they are not being questioned doubtfully or conditionally, but as regards a fact and affirmatively, because, as Seneca has well said: *Qui timide rogat, negare docet.*

First. When the examination takes place in a town in the sierra, the Indian should be asked if he is a *llacuaz* or huari, for they call huari or *llactayoc*[1] anyone native to the town of his ancestors and who have no recollection of having come from outside. All whose fathers and ancestors were born elsewhere they call llacuazes, even if they themselves were born in the town. This distinction is preserved in many districts, and the llacuazes, like persons newly arrived from somewhere else, have fewer huacas. Instead, they often fervently worship and venerate their malquis which, as previously noted, are

[1] *Llactayoc*, a shortened form of *llactacamayoc*, or governor of the people. *Llacta* means city.

the mummies of their ancestors. They also worship *huaris*, that is, the founders of the earth or the persons to whom it first belonged and who were its first populators. These have many huacas and they tell fables about them which furnish much light upon their idolatry. For these and other reasons, there are generally divisions and enmities between the clans and factions and they inform on each other. Thus, we learn about the huacas of both groups, profiting by the occasion when it arises. If one knows to which clan an Indian belongs, he is questioned about this.

Second. What is the name of the principal huaca that you worshiped in this town?

Third. Is the huaca a hill, or crag, or a small stone? And find out as many circumstances and details as possible about it.

Fourth. Has the huaca a son made of stone and considered a huaca like him? Has he a father, brother, or wife? (This question must always be asked, for there are fables about the principal huacas to the effect that they were men, had sons, and were later turned to stone, etc.)

Fifth. Who keeps this huaca?

Sixth. What huacas are most worshiped in this town?

Seventh. Which huacas are worshiped for the fields and for the corn and potatoes? Which huacas do they pray to for the the increase of their herds and the guinea pigs?

Eighth. Whether they have a cocamama or zaramama?

Ninth. What huancas (which are another kind of huaca), called chacrayoc, are worshiped on the farm for its increase?

Tenth. What springs or lagoons are worshiped?

Eleventh. What is the name of your pacarina? —for they generally worship it.

Twelfth. What is the name of your *marcayoc* or *marcachara*? This is a sort of head man or representative of the town. Sometimes it is of stone, at other times the mummy of the ancestor who first populated the land. They are to be asked whether it is a stone or a mummy.

Thirteenth. What is the name of the huaca that is worshiped for rain? This is sometimes a stone, at other times the lightning, although it is sometimes called *llúviac*. They are to be asked whether it is of stone.

Fourteenth. What is the name of the huaca that is worshiped to keep the irrigation ditches from breaking?

Fifteenth. What huaca is worshiped to keep it from raining too much, or to make it rain at the proper time?

Sixteenth. What huaca is worshiped to make the corn grow and keep it from being eaten by worms? From which lagoons do they bring jars of water for the fields and to ask for rain? Into which lagoons do they throw stones to keep them from going dry and to make rain come?

Thirteenth [*sic*]. To which huacas do they offer their newborn twins, called chuchu or curi, or a child born feet first, called chacpa?[2]

Eighteenth. Which huaca is the cacique's, for it is generally the most famous?

Nineteenth. Which huaca is worshiped when they are going to inspect farms, ranches, shops, or mines to insure that they will come back safe and sound? Or which ones to keep the Spaniard from beating them? And what ceremonies they employ in these matters?

Twentieth. They are to ask what the huaca is. Of what sort? How dressed? With what ornaments? And all possible circumstances are to be inquired about and ascertained to keep them from substituting one thing for another and keep them from showing a pretended huaca in order to hide and preserve the true one, as has often happened. Therefore, if possible, one should go to the place where the huaca is.

Twenty-first. What malquis, or mummies of their ancestors, they worship. What their father's name is? How many sons he had? Where they keep them? In what cave or machay, and in what manner?

Twenty-second. What conopa, chanca, or household god they have and whether it is a *micui conopa*, a *zara conopa*,

[2] *Chuchu* or *curi*, see p. 21, n. 21. *Chacpa*, see p. 20, n. 20.

or a *llama conopa;*³ whether it is a conopa of cattle or of corn, and whether the rest of the Indians have one, which is most probable. One has really to insist on this, for it has been found out that they easily reveal common huacas which each one has for his own.

Twenty-third. In order to examine the sorcerer concerning his office, he should be asked whether he is a *víllac*,⁴ or a *huacahuan rímac*, which is the same thing, that is, one who talks to the huaca and gives it offerings, or whether he is a *humu maxa*, who is the most consulted and sought after, or a *rápyac, sácyac, mólcoc,* pachacuc, *azuac,* or *manapac*,⁵ that is, a witch; whether he talks to the Devil, and how he appears to him. Concerning these offices a particular chapter of our story, which is number three, has been written.

Twenty-fourth. They are to be asked about their festivals, when they are celebrated and how, as treated in the fourth chapter, because they differ from place to place. Ask them very privately whether they have confessed to their sorcerers. This, in the Provinces of Cajatambo and Huaylas, is asked thus: *Huachaiquicta aucacucchu canqui?* (Have you confessed your sins to the sorcerers?) And ask them with what ceremonies, as mentioned in Chapter 5.

Twenty-fifth. Ask them on what day they drink, what dances they dance, and what songs they sing during the festivals of the huacas. Ask where they gather to confess to their sorcerers on these days, for there is usually a regular place for this practice, which they call cayan.

Twenty-fifth [*sic*]. Ask whether they keep the mummies of chuchus in their houses (children of one birth), or chacpas

---

³ Penates, *micui conopa, zora conopa* [*sic*], corn totems.

⁴ *Víllac*, priest. *Huacahuarimac* [*sic*], one who talks to the huaca.

⁵ *Humu maxa* should read *humu macsa;* the *macsu* was the privileged male born feet first, who was thought to be predestined to sorcery.

Perhaps *soncoy*, heart, attributing to it the cure of this organ, or an increase of feelings, of which it was supposed to be the center.

Móscoc. That which renews or rejuvenates.

Pachacuc. Divining by means of spiders. See Cobo, *Historia del Nuevo Mundo*, Bk. XIII, Chap. XXXIV (note).

Azuac, chicha[maker].

(children born feet first). Find out who has them and how they died, or, if alive, whether they have been baptized, for usually they have not been.

Twenty-sixth. Ask who cut their child's hair and whether they have kept it, as described in Chapter 6.

Twenty-seventh. Ask about bodies they have disinterred from the church.

Twenty-eighth. Find out about the places called apachita and tocana.[6]

Twenty-ninth. Inquire where and when they worship the sun and the lightning, and which sorcerer is their *lliviac villac,* whose duty it is to invoke it. Find out who is the *malqui villac* of the town.

Thirtieth. Find out whether when they come to the coast they worship snow-covered mountains and the sea by pulling out their eyebrows.

Thirty-first. Ascertain which sorcerers have charge of festivals and fasts and have the chicha prepared, and who teaches the children their idolatry and superstition.

Thirty-second. Ask whether they appoint parianas to guard the fields, and who they are.

Thirty-third. Find out what they offer the huacas and whether the huacas own llamas (which are their sheep) or fields. Learn who is the majordomo of the fields belonging to the huacas, which they call *pachácac.*

Thirty-fourth. Ask the sorcerer what answers he gave the Indians after worshiping the huaca; ask how, when he pretended to talk to the huaca, he became mad (which they often claim). Ask whether it was because of the chicha he drank or the work of the Devil.

Thirty-fifth. Inquire carefully and prudently whether there are any unbaptized persons, because they generally hide a few in order to keep them from baptism, especially those born on the farms and in the country. For it often happens, as I

have seen and have heard Indian women say, when they wish
to be rid of their husbands, that they have not been baptized.
To such a point do their ignorance and malice go.

Thirty-sixth. Finally, they are to be asked what goods their
huaca possesses and whether it has money, which is usually
entrusted to the person who guards it or is kept with the huaca.
Ask whether it has gold or silver, huamas, chacrahincas,
tincurpas, or *aquillas*, from which they give them to drink, for
almost all the huacas have them.

Concerning these and other matters mentioned in this account, which the visitor will have seen and heard, he must
ask the three or four persons just mentioned, as well as some
others whom they will point out. This is not done all at one
time or in haste, but slowly, giving them time to reflect about
what they may have forgotten. To those who know how to
write, paper and ink will be given so that they may write
down what they know. They may also make a quipu for the
purpose or count with corn, which is a common practice among
the Indians. They must also be warned that if huacas are
discovered other than those they have mentioned, or if there
are sorcerers in addition to those they have told about, they
will be punished, etc.

Everything the Indians say should be written down briefly
but clearly and distinctly, and the better for it to be understood, a notebook will be kept for this purpose, bearing the
title: "The Idolatry Discovered in Such a Town, on Such a
Day, in Such a Month and in Such a Year." In the same book
but separately, or in another book, the facts incidentally
discovered about other towns should be written down. Information of this sort and intimations about other places, when
given by the fathers and the visitor, though not strictly a part
of the visit, have been found very useful. For the Indians,
either because they have changed their ways or because they
are being questioned, always tell a great deal. It has also
happened on several occasions that Indians from other places
have come as spies to listen and see what goes on, and by
asking them about huacas in their home towns, much can be

learned about idolatry in distant towns and provinces. At other times, Indians from other places, among them caciques, put in an appearance in order to win the good graces of the visitor, or for other reasons, and they reveal the huacas and sorcerers of their town. Therefore, everything that is found out, by whatever means, should be written down clearly, punctually, and diligently, the certain as certain, the doubtful as doubtful.

In such a way, until experience shows a better one, we commence a visit in towns and provinces that have never experienced one, for these are the most difficult. Let us now see how one should proceed.

CHAPTER SIXTEEN

How a Visit Is to Be Conducted

IN PROVINCES where visits are now being conducted, less effort and diligence are required, and the aforementioned problems are not likely to arise. For the caciques and alcaldes who come to the visitor and to the fathers generally identify their sorcerers without resistance. As already related, within half an hour of our arrival all three hundred and fifty inhabitants of a certain town came to reveal themselves and the alcaldes presented no less than thirty sorcerers and ministers of idolatry. To dispel their fears and win their good will, we treated them kindly, and the visitor gave them a present. It is also useful, before one enters the town to be visited, and as one leaves the previous one, to have some idea of the principal huacas and sorcerers that are to be encountered. With such an opening wedge, the visitor, if he exercises the diligence recommended in the previous chapter, will have little difficulty. For the sorcerers, because of the information that he already has, will either come forward on his arrival or will make themselves known as he reads the edict.

The first thing to be done after the mass and sermon, during which the edict will be read, is to issue an order through the alcaldes and caciques summoning the leading sorcerers of each clan to his quarters. When they have come together, he will give them a brief talk, letting them know that he has come to examine their huacas, rites, and ceremonies. He will treat them with affection on the one hand, at the same time threatening them if they should withhold information. He will set a time limit for them to reflect and to make their quipus. When this is done, each one will be examined separately by the visitor, although it would be useful to have one of the fathers present to help him and to exhort the Indians. In case of necessity, he can also authenticate what is taken down as a notary, assessor, or witness. The town priest, however, should not be present, for with him they are evasive and timid about revealing and declaring themselves. They should be examined according to the questions given in the previous chapter or by asking at least the most essential ones, and, as advised, the visitor will write down everything that is said.

In this fashion the principal sorcerers of the clans, and others whom they mention, will be examined. For this procedure will be helpful in gaining more complete information about the idolatry of the town. The visitor will collect the appropriate information, holding an *auto da fe* for the purpose. For this examination he will call upon the caciques, the leading persons, and two or three additional Indians from each clan, that is to say, the wealthiest and most intelligent ones. He will receive their depositions, remind them solemnly of the gravity of their oath, and urge them to tell the truth. The fathers will aid and abet him in this, and if there are Indians who are literate, each one should bring what he knows in writing. The questions to be asked will either be those already given or at least the following, which are the most essential:

First. Whether there are any Indians in the towns who worship huacas and live in paganism.

Second. Which of the huacas are fixed and which are movable. What malquis they worship. Each clan must tell about its own, and what is said will be written down, in judicial form, viz., that on such a day, in such a month and year, visitor X, having read the edict and having knowledge that in such a town such and such things were declared to exist, in order to ascertain the truth summoned Messrs. X and Y who, having taken an oath in proper form, said that the huacas worshiped in their towns are as follows, etc.

Third. How the aforesaid huacas were worshiped. Whether they were worshiped as gods and creators, whether they were called upon and invoked as *runa camac*[a] and asked for life, health, food, etc.

Fourth. What festivals were celebrated in honor of the aforesaid huacas, at what time of year, and with what rites and ceremonies, fastings, confessions, dancing, and songs.

Fifth. What ministers of idolatry there are in the aforesaid town, unimportant as well as important. And such a man should speak concerning those of his clan, telling of the office that he exercises and the name that he bears.

Sixth. What bodies they know to have been stolen from the church.

Seventh. What wealth the aforesaid huacas possess. Whether they have fields or herds. Whether gold or silver is offered to them, or other objects, as referred to above.

Eighth. Whether they have believed the mysteries of our faith. Ask them about the creation of man and his final end; concerning God in three persons but one in essence; of the coming of Christ Our Lord; of the Holy Sacrament of the Altar; of the adoration of the images; whether they have thought of idolatry as sin; whether they have confessed or have hidden it through fear, etc.

When the aforesaid investigation has been concluded, they will summon all the known ministers of idolatry, whether indicated by the caciques or principal men or because they have come forward and declared themselves, and, taking their oath, the visitor will examine them as he did the preceding persons. Then using the information concerning idolatry

[a] The creator of life.

learned through the statements of one or another, he will advise them in a sermon what it is that they are doing. He will give the whole town to understand the serious crime they have committed in worshiping huacas, etc. He will tell them that they are excommunicated and enemies of God, and that in order to absolve them and lift them out of their sin it will be requisite to examine and question each one separately. They must be earnestly exhorted to tell the truth fearlessly, as they are not to be punished for so doing. They should be warned that no one may tell lies about himself or be guilty of false witness, and that when questioned they should hide nothing, since if they do and it is found out in some manner, they will be punished severely. This must be often suggested and often repeated in the first sermons, and the visitor, the priest, the fathers, and all others who are present in the town must give the Indians much encouragement to reveal themselves and lay aside their fears and embarrassments, however many reasons they have for such feelings. They are to be adjured publicly that each person must reveal his office of sorcerer (if he is one), tell of the huacas and malquis he has worshiped, of the conopas or penates he has in his homes, and of his offerings of mullu, paria, llacsa, *carva, muqui, ato, huahua, sebo,* coca, *sancu,* and the rest of it.

When the mass has been concluded, the visitor will install himself in the church with a table before him and a crucifix or cross on top of it. He will be provided with a blank book for the occasion, different from the one in which he wrote down the idolatry that was discovered. Or, if he uses the same book, he should use a different part of it, giving it this title: "Accusations of the Indians of Such and Such a Town, on such and such a day, month and year." And having the tax list of the town before him, he will call each one by name. Those of each clan will stand outside the church waiting to be examined, and thus standing they will not confuse a legal deposition with the confession. He will question each person briefly: Have you worshiped a huaca? And he will write down what he says. Have you had any dealings with a sorcerer? Have you con-

fessed to him? Have you abstained from salt and pepper?
How many conopas do you have? All these things he will
write down along with the descriptions that are given. What
offerings do you give the huacas? This too he will write down
briefly in this fashion:

"Pedro Paucar worshiped Líbiac, he worshiped it, and
confessed. He has a conopa of black stone shaped like an ear
of corn, or he has a mamazara, mullu, asto, paria, pacto, a
mummified chuchu; he dug up his father's body from the
church."

It is not necessary to find out how often they have worshiped
the huacas, nor any other circumstances, because this procedure is simply for the purpose of finding out whether they
have been idolaters and what things they worship and what
they offer in sacrifices, to deprive them of such things and not,
in this first instance, to punish them. In this the visitor must
be very astute and very precise in order to get them to declare
their conopas, offerings, chuchus and hidden mummies. If they
dissemble, as when a husband reveals what the wife who came
in before him has denied, she must be punished at once. This
can be done by applying a mere twenty lashes on her sheep-
skin or on her yoke pad, or by cutting her hair, not for what
she said but for what she did not say. As the children are
capable of cheating, they should be examined also. It is enough
to ask them whether they have worshiped huacas, confessed,
and fasted in the manner of their paganism. For these three
principles are the first their fathers teach them. Everyone must
submit to this examination, caciques as well as the rest, including the leading persons and sorcerers, summoned according to
the poll list to a place suitable for the purpose. This should be
done even though they have been examined separately, as
described above. The sorcerers may be indicated by a cross
in the margin. The cacique, or leading man of the clan, should
stay there until the examination of his people is finished.
Then he should be told to come in and be examined. If
someone on the poll list is absent, his name should be written
down and a blank of two or three lines left to take down

what he says when he does appear. This examination, at which
it is advisable to have one of the fathers present, but not the
priest, will last until dinner time. Then all those who have
been examined, since no one has been allowed to leave, will
get down on their knees, the men removing the blankets from
their shoulders and the women their llicllas, and stand as a
body outside the church door in two or three rows. The visitor
will then address them, standing at the door of the church,
wearing his surplice and stole and holding two or three staves
in his hand. He will explain to the Indians in a few sober words
that up to now they have been sons of the Devil and in a state
of sin, that they must now be converted in their hearts to the
Lord Our God, and that He will require them to perform acts
demonstrating their error and protesting their conversion to
our faith. They will swear never to leave it, holding the cross
in their upraised right hand. For these outward ceremonies
move the Indians deeply, and long after the visit, when they
go to confession, if asked whether they have again worshiped
huacas they answer: "Since I swore I have never again worshiped a huaca, nor have I had anything to do with sorcerers,
etc." The confessor will then tell them that just as they punish
their children when they are naughty or disobedient, so our
mother church has commanded them to be punished, but
gently, and that they will be whipped with staves in order to
keep them from excommunication. He will explain that even
kings and princes are so treated, using terms that will enable
them to acquire some concept of excommunication. Then he
will absolve them, according to the formula of the Roman
manual or according to that of the *Directorio inquisitorum,*
and this is done at the conclusion, since it is the most solemn
act. All this is necessary if they are to respect ecclesiastical
ceremonies and censures. Then let them enter the church and
have explained to them that what has been done is not the
sacrament of confession, since God has not yet pardoned their
sins. Tell them to confess to the fathers and not to him, as he
is but a judge. After this the visitor will present two or three
brief arguments. When the bell rings at two-thirty in the

afternoon, this interrogation and examination are continued until sunset. And at the conclusion absolution is given, as has been observed. While the examinations are going on, confession can also be in progress, especially for the unmarried men and women who have no conopas to exhibit nor offerings nor other objects of worship like the rest. Usually, however, it is advisable for them to make confession after they have surrendered the objects mentioned during the examination.

When these interrogations have been concluded, the visitor will order the sorcerers and the leading men of the clan who have revealed the existence of the huacas to go out and fetch them. It seems proper that this should occur before their abjuration and solemn absolution. This is the principal purpose of the visit, and in it much care and diligence must be exercised, for it has often happened that the Indians hide the really important huacas and substitute other stones for them. For this reason, it is essential to have descriptions of the huacas and of the places where they are located. For the same reason the visitor himself, a priest, or some trustworthy person must go with the sorcerers, and scarcely any Indian can be trusted to do this. The journey is always difficult, and sometimes one has to go on foot on very bad roads. Whoever goes with them should be provided with a list of the huacas and malquis, and with it as many precise indications and descriptions as possible. He must bear an order to destroy the places of worship and the machays and to place large crosses where the principal huacas were. He should also command all dead bodies that have been dug up to be returned to the church.

When all this has been accomplished, a day should be appointed, at as early a date as possible, for the display of the huacas. The Indians will be warned of this in sermons and catechisms, and a proclamation will be made the night before. For in addition to the conopas, mamazaras, axomamas, paria, llacsa, coca, and other offerings, they will also bring chuchus, chacpas, and pacto, and all the drums, tumblers, jars, and containers used to give food and drink to their huacas. They must also bring the pots in which they brew their tecti or chicha for the huacas, the jugs they carry it in, the animal skins and staffs of the parianas, the *quepas* or trumpets and horns and other objects with which they served the huacas, and especially the shirts of cumbi or, if they have them, those called *humaras,*[b] and which many important Indians wear. These last it is not well to deprive them of unless they are used only for the huacas. They should be impressed with the fact that these objects are taken away from them on account of their idolatry and not simply to take advantage of them, which last would be most improper. They will also be told to bring wood for the burning.

The next day the bell will ring very early, and when mass has been said (because on this day there can be no sermon), the whole town will assemble in the square by clans, bringing with them and carrying on their person everything that they are to exhibit and declare before the visitor. They are to be called upon according to the tax list, in the order in which they were examined. Each one should bring what he said he possessed and what was written down by the visitor at the time of the examination. Everything that they bring is to be written down, not in the book in which individual examinations were recorded, but in the book of interrogation in which the confessions of the sorcerers and leading men of the clan were registered. Great care must be exercised in this to keep them from hiding anything, for they will do so if they can. Public punishment should be given to anyone who hides anything.

After the individuals have given up their objects, the sorcerers are to hand over the huacas and malquis that they are in charge of and which they have brought from their hiding places, and the name and face of huacas that each one hands over is to be recorded.

These things, which are generally numerous even in small towns, are to be piled up outside the town together with the mummies of malquis removed from the church and burned in a large bonfire in a remote place. I know a town, and not a very large one, where on such an occasion more than three

[b] A sleeveless shirt.

hundred objects were burned at one time. The aquillas,° drinking vessels, trumpets, and huamas and other objects of silver, even though of little worth, are weighed and counted in these public exhibitions, to be accounted for in the judicial proceeding to those who are to receive them. Therefore, the visitor and the fathers present sign these lists, as it is more important than is generally understood for the Indians to perceive and be persuaded that there is no intention during a visit of taking away from them anything that is rightfully theirs, but only objects which are without profit to anyone, hurtful to all, and an offense to the Lord Our God because they are used in the service and ministry of the huacas. This demonstration must be so conducted that no one, however ill intentioned, whether present or absent, can blame the visitor or his office in any way. Some persons have indeed tried to do so against all reason and truth, and the defense has been, and must always be, the truth and creditable witnesses to it.

The following day everything left over from the fire is gathered and, for the reasons already given, disposed of in the manner prescribed in the first chapter. But I must again give warning, because of what has happened after a visit in many places, that although it requires effort to do so, everything which would not burn in the fire must be thrown away where it can never be found. If possible, the Indians should be prevented from seeing this done and from knowing where the material has been thrown. As the Lord Archbishop has ordered, everything that has been placed under the crosses near the church should, when a good occasion offers, be taken out, dissipated, scattered, and thrown into the river, where there will remain neither memory nor trace of it. For a few months ago sacrifices of guinea pigs and other things habitually offered to the huacas were found around the cross beneath which the residue from the burned huacas had been buried.

When the exhibitions are over, the visitor should gather the sorcerers together at his house on a convenient day and inquire again about their offices, writing their replies down in the

° Tumbler, drinking vessel.

account. At this time he should sentence them to come to Christian teaching every morning and afternoon; they may not be absent without the priest's permission. They should wear around their necks a wooden cross about six inches long, and he will tell them to mend their ways and threaten them with punishment unless they do so, and so forth. This done, a suitable day should be set for the festival of the cross, to be celebrated whenever it can be done with most solemnity, as for instance at vespers, with a chanted mass. The streets will be prepared for a procession in which a mounted statue of the crucified Christ, or a crucifix, will be carried on a feretory[d] under a canopy.

Before mass the Indians are to assemble in some place that has been previously announced. From there they will carry the large cross or image to the church, but without the canopy. The sorcerers are to go in a body with candles in their hands and a cord around their necks, and the most guilty ones should wear hair shirts and will attend mass ahead of all the others. When the sermon is over, the leading ministers of idolatry, who have been coached beforehand, are to stand on the steps of the altar or in some high place, and one after another each one will address the townspeople, saying that he has deceived and betrayed them, that all that he has told them was a lie, that henceforth he will not summon them to make sacrifices to the huacas, etc.

At the conclusion of the mass, there will be a procession, and the litany of the cross will be sung in the Indian language (which has been printed), and at the end of the procession the sorcerers will march like penitents in front of the statue that is born aloft. This spectacle will arouse in those who look upon it as they should much devotion and deep feeling. It has been ordered that this festival is to be celebrated solemnly in all towns on September 14, the day of the Exaltation

---

[d] *En andas.* A troublesome expression because, since the custom of carrying statues about in public processions is not practiced in the United States, words and phrases to translate it are hard to find. Father Feinman of Louisville, Kentucky, suggested *feretory,* which is in the dictionary but which is rarely used. *Supra,* p. 95.

of the Cross, or on the following Sunday, in memory of the mercy Our Lord has shown them by leading them out of their errors and idolatry. For the same reason, a cross to commemorate the day will be most carefully raised in the plaza of the town.

On the festival of the cross, or on a later day, whichever is more convenient, either before or after mass, the regular statutes and ordinances for the remedy of idolatry, to be found at the end of this account, are to be read and explained, adding in each town such details as appear necessary there. These statutes are to be written down in the book of the church with a list of the huacas and the names of the sorcerers who were present. They are also to be listed on a tablet to be placed on the church publicly, giving the offices held by each one, so that the priest may pay particular attention to them. For the Lord Archbishop, after consultation, has decided that the memory of the sorcerers and of the huacas should remain public along with the town's superstitions, to be inscribed in a book which the priest will keep, so that he will know which errors he has to refute.

The consolation and contentment of the Indians when the visit is over cannot be told, but must be felt and seen to be appreciated. This is not because the visitor is leaving, but through the realization of their own deceits and for having been taught and confessed. It is true that this delight, contentment, and disenchantment is mainly exhibited by the common people of the town, children and adults, as they were the ones who were deceived. Many of the old people, however, see themselves pointed out and affronted, as they have lost their credit and prestige with the rest. They feel their loss of status most keenly, for they have been separated from the use and exercise of their offices and pagan ministries. They are also so used to, so wrapped up in the love of their huacas, idolatries, superstitions, and ceremonies, that they find all the more strange and alien the love and knowledge of the mysteries of our faith and all the other aspects of the Christian religion. For this reason, some of them are but barely undeceived, and it is easy for them to return to their errors, and they are nothing loath to take with them as many as they can, teaching them and exercising again their offices and ministries. The rest are readily enlightened and more constant in the truth they have learned, and they show much gratitude to the fathers, begging them to come back and asking them when they will do so. And when they do return to a village, they are received with extraordinary signs of joy. But if the joy of the Indians is great, greater still is the joy of the persons who have taught and confessed them, seeing how different the town is from the way they found it—on its way to eternal life *ut cognoscant te Deum verum, et quem misisti Iesum Christum.*

CHAPTER SEVENTEEN

Conclusion and Summary of Everything
That Has Been Said

IN THE PROLOGUE we proposed to divide this treatise into three parts. The first was concerned with showing what huacas and idols the Indians worship, what they give them as offerings, what festivals they celebrate for them, what abuses and superstitions they have, and what priests, teachers, and ministers of idolatry there are. The second was to treat the causes and roots thereof, why on the one hand they were so well hidden, why they flourished, and what the remedies are to uncover and uproot them. The third, what method and practice of visits is the best and most immediate means of doing so.

I have done what I set out to do (if I am not mistaken). At least, I am sure that I have wanted to accomplish my purpose and that I have tried to do so. There are two things left for me to speak of: first, the state of matters today, at the beginning of Lent in the year 1621, and the means already described for the remedy of the evils; second, what means are most necessary, suitable, and efficacious. Let me begin by saying that the means to be employed and executed are many and various.

Some of the means have to do with the princes and rulers, secular as well as ecclesiastic, who order them carried out. Others have to do with those who execute them. Some are means of universal application and others are particular ones, some immediate and some less so, some more, and some less efficacious, some are for all time and others for a limited time. The reader can decide which means are pertinent for him and which should be preferred in theory as well as in execution. It has not been my intention to write a treatise like that written by a worthy person such as Father Acosta, of our Society, *De Procurando salute Indorum,* or the barefoot Carmelite, Father Friar Thomas of Jesus, *De Procurando salute omnium gentium.* I should like everyone to read their books, for I am certain they would be singularly profitable. The beginning and foundation of this whole edifice is to furnish some idea and some proper opinion of the malady and the knowledge of it which its seriousness requires. If those who are legally obliged to action, as we are all morally so obliged, do their duty, then the medicine which the illness demands will be applied.

This obligation is required of everyone, though not in equal degree. Even those who by reason of their state have retired from the world and been forgotten by it are not free from it. Let them all hear the admirable words of Saint John Chrysostom, in the prayer of Saint Philogonius, which, in order not to deprive his words of their force, although it is even greater in Greek, I shall quote in Latin: "Nulla prorsus alia res est, quae perinde declaret, doceatque quis sit fidelis, et amans Christi, quam si fratrum curam gerat, proque illorum salute gerat solicitudinem. Haec omnes audiant, etiam Monachi, qui montium occuparunt acumina, quique modis omnibus se ipsos crucifixerunt quo pro viribus Ecclesiarum Praefectos adiuvent, horumque causas leniant precibus, concordia, charitate," etc.

But the unique, the principal remedy for this evil, and the cure for this infirmity, is to be found among the priests and depends on their zeal. There is no little mystery in the fact that the word *care* should be the same as *priest* and *priest* another word for *care.*[a] I say they are the only remedy because everything else, even if put into practice, will not accomplish so much as they can accomplish alone. The priests bear the *pondus diei, et aestus* to cultivate this uncultivated vine which the Hound of Hell[b] is trying so hard to destroy. One can repeat with reason the words of Psalm 79: *Exterminavit eam aper de silva, et singularis ferus depastus est eam.* The priests, as Saint Bernard said of Saint Peter with regard to the whole church, uphold the part with which the Lord has charged them: *oratione, exemplo, et doctrina.* They are to negotiate the winning of souls for heaven with holy desires, fervent prayer, and overflowing tears. Prayer will give them a sense of their value, will put fire into their words, and will find a thousand ways of winning. Without prayer and without a sense of the value of the soul, fervent sermons and efficient means will be as little or nothing. And if prayer is important, example is no less so for the conversion of souls. The Indians often look at our hands, for neither they nor even the Spaniards can distinguish what Christ Our Lord said of those who sit in Moses' seat: *Quaecunque dixerint vobis servate et facite, secundum vero opera eorum nolite facere.* They do more quickly what they have seen us do than what they have heard us say. As Saint Leo the Pope said: *Fortiore sunt exempla quam verba.* He who teaches with deeds and words works with two hands as did those who rebuilt Jerusalem; as the Scripture says, II Esdras 4: *Una manu faciebant opus, et altera tenebant gladium;* or as those spoken of in Judges 20: *Erant viri fortissimi, ita sinistra, ut dextra praeliantes;* and Joshua [Judges] 3, speaking in high praise of Ehud: *Suscitavit eis salvatorem Aod, qui*

---

[a] An untranslatable pun. Latin *cura* means priest or care in Spanish, though in the latter use it has been mainly replaced in modern Spanish by *cuidado.*

[b] *Jabalí,* wild boar. Hound is our usual word in this expression.

utraque manu pro dextera utebatur.[c] A word accompanied by deed is worth more than many without it. This is the model: *Princeps pastorum cœpit JESUS facere, et docere.* The visitors and men of religion who go out on missions to teach the Indians accomplish a great deal, but the pasturing and watering by their priests is what does most good, continuing with sermons on all feast days of obligation, with Christian teaching on Wednesdays and Fridays, with ordinary catechisms, and even ordinary conversations in season and out. We must talk of our faith, our ecclesiastical history, the lives of the saints, which they greatly enjoy hearing, refuting their errors and teaching our truths until they are thoroughly convinced of both.

Another way to uproot idolatry and plant the faith among the Indians is for the curacas and caciques to become what they ought to be. Whose duty is it to make this possible, who is most able to do this, and who is most accustomed to doing this, but their priests? I say the same thing about making it easy for them to send their children to the boarding schools and to appreciate the kindness that His Majesty is doing them in this.

Who except the priests can rid them of their drunkenness, which creates, foments, and preserves their idolatry? Who else can deal with them in a kindly and gentle manner and then in a harsh way, meting out punishment? The priests should be the immediate executors of everything said here that pertains to the commands of the Lord Viceroy and the Lord Archbishop. They must tend those who relapse into idolatry, particularly the known ministers and teachers of idolatry, and must teach them, to keep them from returning to their ministry. Those who are most harmful must be sent into custody, and no one can do this better than the priests.

The repair of the churches, the decoration of the altars, the adornment of the statues, the richness of the ornamentation, the variety of music, the care of divine worship, the celebration

[c] The modern Vulgate text reads: suscitavit eis salvatorem vocabula Ahoth filium Gera filii lemini qui utraque manu utebatur pro dextera.

of the festivals, the understanding of the confession, and the reverence of the Most Blessed Sacrament are all important, and the most efficacious means of improving the Christian religion is to have good, saintly, diligent priests, learned especially in theology. For it is wrong to say and believe that theology is not necessary for the Indians, as is commonly said in Peru. As Saint Jerome has well observed, the ABC's and the spelling out of the alphabet inform a literate man differently from one who knows no more than that. And to teach a little it is important for the teacher to know a great deal. This is all the more true since there is nothing more important than the mysteries of our faith, or more difficult to have understood by those who understand material and ordinary things only. The importance of this point is well known, for it sums up all the rest, and the Lord Viceroy, by privilege of rank, chooses from among the many those who are excellent, those who he thinks are outstanding, without reference to person, without yielding to special pleading, and in this manner he gives rewards and promotions to those who have worked among the Indians. Many pertinent examples of this could be adduced if desirable.

Sometimes it has seemed to me that if having taught Christian doctrine to the Indians were not merely a consideration, but a *sine qua non* for election or promotion to ecclesiastical livings and benefices—or at the very least a distinct advantage and a help—more learned men would deign to learn the language and not dismiss it as a matter of little importance. At the same time, those who already know it would be encouraged to continue their studies and as a result their theological knowledge would improve, and they would enjoy books more. It would be most helpful if all priests could be of the sort we have been talking about, the kind of men they ought to be, and if the usual visitors were equally worthy and possesed of zeal for the well-being of the Indians. They have got to know the language, for, as has been observed in its proper place, it is their responsibility to see whether the priests can speak it, to examine and approve the sermons that have been preached and that are supposed to have been written down.

It is up to them to honor, to favor, and to accredit worthy priests in every way possible, not merely with the towns but with their superiors in the hierarchy. For all the honor we can give to the priests, all the favor that can be shown to them, all the interest that we can have in them is little enough. The work they do, the solicitude and care which they display, the very danger to their lives in which good priests find themselves as they perform their duties by day and by night deserve nothing less. In them are surely summed up all the possible means of Christianizing the Indians. Let us now see the state in which the Prince of Esquilache has left them today as he returns to Spain.

CHAPTER EIGHTEEN

Remedies for the Extirpation of Idolatry in This Archbishopric and How They Now Stand at the Beginning of Lent, 1621

IN THIS ARCHBISHOPRIC, where so much energy has been expended to uproot idolatry, there are still towns and no few of them that have yet to be visited for the first time, although many, as has been noted, have been visited twice. It was about three weeks ago that three fathers left to accompany Master Julián de los Ríos, of the province of Checras, on a visit. At the time he was at his mission with no expectation of being called, but he was sent out with title of visitor to the province of Chinchacocha and other places, because his superiors were satisfied that he would do a good job. The outcome of this mission cannot yet be reported, but it is possible to express the hope that its conclusion will be as excellent as its beginning has been laborious. Yesterday we heard in a letter of the dangers from which the Lord Our God has saved them on the highway. One of the fathers had fallen twice and was caught by the stirrup under a mule in a narrow place. The mule of the other father, who was walking and leading him with his right hand, fell down a hill. Such occurrences are so common they no longer even surprise us.

The day before the three fathers had set out, two others left to go with Dr. Alonso Osorio to continue the visit in the *corregidor* district of Huarochirí which is closer to here than to Lima. It began about three months ago but was interrupted by the Christmas season. Yesterday this letter came from a place about twelve leagues away.

Today, January 24, I am ending my work in the town of X, where the Indians have been so persistent in their idolatry that almost all of them have relapsed into paganism, have been celebrating the festival of the huacas as before, and have removed the crosses placed over them. They had hidden twenty malquis, which I found and burned, and three principal huacas. They were consulting their priests, of whom eight were left. Two of these went to the city and I have sent for them. Six exhibited their conopas and their divining stones used for casting lots. They confessed their crimes and I sentenced them to the house of Santa Cruz. The help of the fathers has been needed to find out what has been found out. We shall send in an account of all this, of the additional huacas that have been found, and even of some things yet unheard of, as our work is concluded. Let me simply say this for now: in this province of Huarochirí, and in all its towns, they celebrate a festival and assembly of the population called a Huatanchana. It takes place in May or June and lasts three days. During this celebration they describe in order the faults that they have committed during the year, such as not obeying their curacas, not doing their assigned work, being lazy, and not appealing to their huacas. The chief priest holds in his hand a thin strand of yarn, in lieu of a whip. After he has sacrificed to Chaupinámoc, the sister of the idol Pariacaca, both of which are famous in this province, he strikes them with the yarn and they are absolved. I shall write later of the peculiar observances of this festival and of many other things.

As one travels through this province, a visit and mission must go to Huamalíes, which is the last town in the archbishopric and greatly in need of reform. Last year Dr. Hernando de Avendaño began to

conduct a visit there. Later on the remaining provinces of this archbishopric will have to be visited in their turn, but this will be the
work of years.

This same Dr. Avendaño is now commencing his visit to the
Indians of the city of Lima, and this week he has taken over
the curacy of the cathedral. It is well understood that this
city, as head of the kingdom and the center of Christianity,
will require less reform than other places. It is to be feared,
nevertheless, that no little idolatry will be encountered, and
even somewhat more in the surrounding territory, as time will
tell and experience teach.

To avoid difficulties in continuing these missions, the com-
plement of mules and other necessary equipment which His
Excellency the Viceroy donated at the outset are being kept
and repaired with alms given for the purpose, for ordinarily
no less than six fathers go on a mission together. The Lord
Archbishop has also helped with large offerings for the purchase of rosaries, images, and other objects of devotion to be
divided among the Indians during the missions. The fathers
always accept from His Lordship whatever is offered. Very
adequate commissions and decrees are provided the visitors
so as to give them recourse to secular justice, if need be, speci-
fying serious penalties for those who fail to obey. They have
the right to send to the coast to the house of detention the
Indians who do most harm, and, within the limits of the decree,
they may send to boarding school all the sons of the caciques.

They call this institution the School of the Prince, not so
much because it was donated by the Prince of Esquilache, but
because it has been placed under the protection and sponsor-
ship of His Highness Prince Don Felipe, may he live long and
happily. For its patron in heaven it has B. P. Francisco de
Borja, as has been established in its constitution and in the
decree that founded it. About thirty sons of caciques are
enrolled there at present. They are dressed in the uniform
and clothing that have already been described in their proper
place. They sleep together and eat together, and are read to
at table in the presence of the father rector of the school, who

takes his meals with them. The latter has been the rector of several schools, including the principal ones of our Society in this province, and has served in its principal offices. A father of our Society teaches the boys to read, write, and count, and a choirmaster teaches them to sing. In the church are many talented musicians, vocal as well as instrumental. The day is divided so as to provide time for all these occupations, and the boys are given lectures and conversations suited to their age and capacity dealing with Christian doctrine, the mysteries of the faith, and the principles of good conduct. They also have hours for mass, rosary, examination of conscience, and other devotions. Days are set apart for Christian teaching, the confessional, and for taking Communion. Our purpose is to teach them to work and to develop into the kind of men they should be. We will pluck the finest fruit when these tender plants come to bloom, yet we enjoy them already though they are but in flower, as I shall now explain.

A cacique nearby brought up his son so neglectfully that to describe it would arouse as much pity as wonder. In order to get the son into school, the Viceroy had to order his father to be brought in as a prisoner. Within a few days, using a poor excuse and much pleading, he took him away again, and to prevent his return to school he married him off. This despite the fact that he was only fourteen years old at the time, if my information is correct. His Excellency ordered him returned to school in spite of his marriage. The boy was so insolent and rebellious that he had to be handcuffed. I interceded for him and the father rector agreed to take the handcuffs off him if he would learn his Christian doctrine, of which he knew not one word. In four or five days he had learned the whole of it to the point of being able to assist at mass, etc.

In the house of detention at Santa Cruz, which is used for the most harmful teachers and ministers of idolatry, there are about forty men at present, most of them advanced in years. The house was built for this purpose and can hold a great many persons. The men are allowed out only on feast days to hear mass and the sermon and to march in a procession with their crown agents. A Jesuit father teaches them Christian doctrine every day. By the Viceroy's orders they are given enough to eat and are furnished the means to spin wool, an easy task much practiced by the Indians. With this work they earn their food, which costs little, and get spending money, and all who are able to work and want to do so are provided with the means to do it.

An honorable and trustworthy Spaniard is in charge of the business affairs of the house and provides the food and the wool for the spinning. He also collects what has been spun. He sees to it that the ill are taken care of and keeps those who are well from escaping. A fair number of them have managed to do this, and even though the walls are high and thick, some men have tried to break through. Those who are detained for a limited time only may go home when their time is up. The rest leave when they are thought to be cowed enough, reformed enough, and well enough taught. But as most of them are past eighty, many have died, after having been given the sacraments, which is no small sign of their predestination. While still in detention, some of the men have been moved by the Lord Our God to reveal the huacas that they left hidden in their towns, and I have their depositions in my possession. Others have been ordered back from their district to tell where they have left them. Such was the case of two men whom the Licentiate Rodrigo Hernández Príncipe wrote about, hoping they would reveal their secrets here and become disillusioned, thereby placing themselves on the road to salvation. The people of their town had accused them of having merely given up a few huacas while failing to reveal the principal ones. Yesterday, February 5, another old Indian, being ill and exhausted and without hope of life, called in one of our fathers and asked him to write down an account of what he had left hidden, which had to do with huacas, because he wished to die like a good Christian, etc. Among the things he said was that the house containing the idols and the silver they had should be used for the Most Blessed Sacrament. He also requested that a well-carved stone to be found there should be made into a font for holy water. I have this account in my possession to entrust to any person who will carry out its dictates. I have given these details in order to demonstrate how deep is the old men's love for their huacas and how important it is to remove them from where they are doing so much harm.

Before concluding this chapter there are matters which, if I would not hurt truth and reason, I must tell. As noted at the outset, Dr. Alberto de Acuña, judge of this Royal Audience, is a man who gives encouragement to everything that has to do with the increase of Christianity among the Indians and who encourages all the abovementioned measures designed for that purpose. It is to him, because of his zeal for the well-being of the Indians and his intelligence in the government of this kingdom, that His Excellency forwards most matters that pertain to the natives. He then proposes suitable means for lessening difficulties that arise, satisfies the doubts of serious persons who are unacquainted with the facts, points out the reality of the situation, and answers objections and calumnies that arise. He has responsibility for promulgating the statutes and for the founding of the boarding schools. He is responsible for the various decrees that have been issued from time to time, for the letters to the prelates, *corregidors*, caciques, and all others in this realm. He frequently visits the school of the caciques and attends to their wants with affection. He stoops to insignificant details as if each boy were his own son. It is not surprising that he should treat the caciques in this manner, for he acts no differently toward the sorcerers, visiting them with the same solicitude and attention, inquiring whether their needs are provided for and asking them in kindly fashion whether they need anything. He often neglects important business having to do with his own household and office in order to give attention to these troublesome and difficult problems, since all these matters have to do with the service of Our Lord, from whom alone a reward can be expected.

Such is the state of affairs with regard to Christianity among the Indians of this archbishopric. Let us now see how matters stand in places outside of it and in the remainder of Peru.

CHAPTER NINETEEN

The State of Christianity outside This Archbishopric and in the Rest of Peru

A NYONE who has read thus far, especially if he comes from outside this kingdom, would, I believe, like to know how Christianity fares in provinces and bishoprics other than this.

It can be said, in a word, that the area under discussion is the best and the most cultivated region, whether already visited or in the process of being visited, and that its condition is as already described. From this it can be imagined what the rest of the country must be like. But in order that the situations may be more easily comprehended, let me tell the story in its outlines, retracing my steps a little. Let me begin by saying that this fourth part of the world which we call America, in honor of Americo Vespucci, its discoverer, omitting the many islands that lie ahead of it, is divided into two principal land areas, one called New Spain, or the kingdom of Mexico, and the other Peru. Each one contains many kingdoms and provinces populated by numerous and diverse nations, some more and some less barbarous, some more and some less civilized. These two parts are divided from each other by a strait of land whose Greek name, also used among the Romans, is an isthmus. On this isthmus, toward the Northern Sea, is the city and stronghold of Puertobello, and rightly so named.[a] Toward the Southern Sea is the city of Panama, rendered noble by its Royal Audience and bishopric, and situated at approximately 8 degrees north latitude, 85 degrees longitude.

Between Puertobello and Panama the isthmus is eighteen leagues wide. From Panama one goes by land, continuing up the river Chagres, which flows into the sea a little above Puertobello at a place we call Cruces. From there it is six

---

[a] Beautiful port. In this instance it is spelled with one *l* in the Spanish edition, elsewhere with two. The latter form is correct.

leagues by land to Panama. If this land bridge were not there, there would be two great islands, New Spain to the north, and this great kingdom of Peru. The latter begins at Panama and broadens out from 50 degrees longitude where the coast of Brazil is extended. And before this latter kingdom, which belongs to the crown of Portugal, the land continues down the coast to where two of the world's greatest rivers run, the Marañón and the Orellana, flowing into the Northern Sea. From Brazil it continues along the coast of Buenos Aires to the great Río de la Plata all the way down to the Straits of Magellan. Along the coast of the Western Sea, it broadens out to 89 degrees longitude at its widest part on the coast at Trujillo, at 8 degrees south latitude, and runs all the way from Lima, which is at 12½ degrees and is the most populated place in Peru. At 34 degrees south latitude, toward the kingdom of Chile, this new world becomes narrower toward the Straits of Magellan, as was discovered ninety years ago. At its middle it is located at 80 degrees, more or less, longitude and is prolonged to 53 degrees latitude or distance from the Antarctic pole. These are the extremes on the two sides of this wide kingdom, whose phenomena, natural as well as moral, are so extraordinary. Much has been written about it, but there remains a long and no less pleasant story to be told about it.

Almost in the middle of the continent from north to south, from its beginning to the Straits of Magellan, run high sierras which are here called the cordillera, which widens sometimes and then narrows again, leaving warm and fertile valleys in some places, and in other places extensive cold plains, and in still other places mountains of colder climate, which we call the sierra. In some areas these mountains are so high that they are covered with eternal snow. In others there are places we call punas that are useful only as cattle pasture or for the vicuñas, which are like mountain goats. In their stomachs a kind of stone is found,[b] and from their wool is made the

<hr />

[b] In English, cattlemen call this a hairball. They sometimes attain a stonelike consistency.

finest cumbi, which can compete with the damasks of Europe. The areas that slope from the sierras to the Southern Sea we commonly call the lowlands, although they are so only in name. This is the land most dwelt in by the Spaniards, and the Indians there are stronger and more energetic than those of the sierra.

All the provinces that lie within the cordillera and its slopes toward the Southern Sea are populated by Christian Indians or, to speak more accurately, baptized Indians. This is also true of those on the slopes that fall toward the Northern Sea. A few leagues away, however, are vast mountains and forests, though the land is less rugged than that of the sierra, and in many areas there are great plains we call pampas. And both mountain ranges are commonly called the Andes, and they are populated by nations who have never seen the light of the Gospel. These Indians often come out to barter or to exchange goods with the Spaniards and Christian Indians. These provinces take the name of cities that are within their borders, such as Chuquiavo where, in the province of Chunchos, a few years ago, they killed Father Miguel de Urrea, of our Society. He had come to those places, including those we went into in the year 1584, preaching to those nations. Near Cuzco and Huamanga there are other entrances to the Andes through which two fathers of our Society tried to penetrate for the conversion of those nations, but after much hard work they came out unsuccessful. In the city of Huánuco, which is also on the north slope and a part of this archbishopric, is one of the finest climates in the world. Its temperature is so uniform that the fruit trees bear in all seasons and flowers there grow in a profusion. And close to where they are winnowing wheat, another crop is being sown and a field lies fallow. This is close to the land of the Panataguas Indians. Some of the latter came while I was at the mission in the city and asked that they and their children be baptized. The province of Huamalíes, which is also in this archbishopric, has in it the Carapachas Indians who often venture out, especially at the festival of Corpus Christi, into the Christian towns to get various goods that cannot be found elsewhere. Last year, while Dr. Hernando de Avendaño was visiting the town of Huacaibamba, eighteen of them came out together, and with them an Indian woman who had been raised in Huánuco and knew Spanish. They asked to be made Christians and begged the fathers to come and build churches there. He catechized them through an interpreter because the visitor did not speak Quechua. He gave them some notion of the mysteries of our faith, particularly about the immortality of the soul and the glory of the blessed, and he made them all so content and happy that they jumped for joy, with special signs of rejoicing and jubilation, clapping their hands and speaking in their language. When the visitor asked through the interpreter why they did that, he said it was for joy that their souls would not die, but that as they were good Christians they would go to Heaven.

A few months before, when the Licentiate Miguel Rubio was a priest in the same town, he spent three days in the company of other Indians who had come there. Part of the journey had to be covered on foot, and part of the way they carried him on their shoulders. He stayed with them three or four days and two leading Indians gave him their sons of about fifteen years of age to be taught and baptized. One of these boys died soon after being baptized, and he brought the other to Lima. There I kept him in our house, and in a little while he had learned the common language of the Indians, and with it the Christian doctrine. But he fell ill on the very day of his baptism and died serene and content because he said he was going to Heaven. God has a thousand ways to accomplish the good of his predestined and we experience this in myriad ways each day.

Many nations are also found in the provinces of Chachapoyas and Moyobamba and during recent years attempts have been made to populate the land between them. Within the bishopric of the city of Quito, which, because it is below the line, is rather cold, many other nations are found. Father Rafael Ferrer of our Society, who went to them with the news of the Gospel, was killed by the Cofan Indians not many years ago. And we have knowledge of many other nations, although not all of them have been discovered. Many leagues lie between what has been discovered, in the direction of the Northern Sea, on the coast of Brazil, and so on, as already observed, in the aforementioned cordillera which traverses all of Peru. In addition, there are other and easier points of entry through the provinces of Tucumán and Paraguay. Some fathers from Brazil met some of those from this province a few years ago and traveled about for a long time teaching those nations. At present, a province of our Society, distinct from this one, maintains the houses in Chile, Tucumán, and Paraguay. They have brought thousands of Indians to the Christian church, and they keep them with much effort, although they must endure great poverty to do so. Of this much could be said, but He who rewards knows all about it. In those regions other nations are being discovered and this is no less true in the jurisdiction of the Holy Cross of the sierra. Let us therefore say: *Rogate Dominum messis, ut mittat operarios in vineam suam.* Close by, in the well-known land of Potosí, are the Chiriguanaes Indians, who provide no little cause for observation. Not only are they non-Christians, but they are so bold and insolent that those in neighboring lands live in abject terror of them. Their frightful raids do much damage and are an affront to the Spaniards. This was shown last month when they attacked the valleys of Pazpaya and Pilaya. The *corregidor* of Potosí himself went out against them with two hundred men to hold the pass and, in case they tried to advance, to force them to retreat. In the new part of the kingdom where the archbishopric of Santa Fe is located, the need is great as it is here. It is true that in years gone by the Indians were deprived of their huacas and idols, which were many and various. The Lord Archbishop Don Bartolomé Guerrero worked there in person. He was then archbishop of Santa Fe, but now he holds that office in this city. There is also understood to be much need in the bishopric of Quito. To prove this I need present no other testimony than two letters which I have. They came from an Indian governor of some towns who, because he was raised in this city, has a suitable knowledge of the Christian religion and a hatred of the errors of the Indians. Those deceptions are the same as those I discovered and experienced in the coastal towns more than two hundred leagues away, which is where these letters come from. He writes in Spanish and with very good handwriting. I shall quote him without changing a word. His letter is addressed to Father Joan Vázquez, principal of the boarding school for the caciques, and it came into my hands this week. After his first chapter, consisting of greetings and salutations, he says:

My second reason for writing is to discharge my conscience and see if the hand of Your Reverence can castigate the errors, sorcery, and *padrejonerías* (for in that province the masters of idolatry and sorcerers are called *padrejones*, just as in Huamanga they are called *licenciados*) to be found in my jurisdiction, which are a disgraceful and sorrowful thing to see. Whenever some poor Indian bandies words with one of these he soon kills him, and there is no remedy, for it is done at night when they wander about as they like. Since Your Reverence is such a good Christian, let him have a decree sent to the place where these ministers of idolatry are, because, as I say, the Indians pray to God for a remedy.

When one of the Indians is dying after an injury inflicted by one of them, he seems clearly to see the offender and says: "Take So-and-So away from me for he is near me." And he says this when no one is present save his own relations. As his governor I list the following names for Your Reverence, omitting many others who could be named, so that they may be removed from here without further investigation. And if this is done, it must be done at night gently and with kindness, for most of the Indians in this town are both shrewd and patriotic, etc.

At this point he names individuals, and of one of them he says: "He killed the most Indians in his town." And after a few days he wrote another letter to the same effect.

In another part of this archbishopric, near the city of Jaén, about 4 degrees latitude from this center, Governor Don Diego Vaca went in with his people about two years ago to the territory of the Maina, Jíbaro, and Cocamama Indians, who had settled on the banks of the Marañón River. There he discovered many thousands of Indians, some of them peaceful, and because the land is rich in gold, a useful door is open for the conversion of these pagans. Few there are who wish to visit the pagans except through the door of gold and silver.

The kingdom and provinces of Peru are divided into three archbishoprics and sixteen bishoprics, and some of the churches were built for them some years ago. The most important church, that of Lima, has had but two prelates, and the present one, who has been there many years, is the third. It was erected in twenty-two days in the month of January 1535, when the first stone was laid for the founding of this city. In these eighty-five years it has grown so considerably that it can compete in every way with many in Europe. The people are not numerous, for there cannot be more than twelve thousand Spaniards, either from Spain or born here, about eleven thousand Negroes, including those who arrive every year from Guinea, and those born here, and a little more than two thousand Indians. There are also those who are a mixture of the three races to an extent that varies with the individual—in all, about thirty thousand people.

Many factors render the city illustrious, such as the continued presence of the viceroy and the chancellery, the fact that it is a bishopric and holds the primacy of the region, the fact that the court of the inquisition with its vast jurisdiction is located here, and the presence of the university, which is unique in the kingdom. The students of the university are not numerous in comparison with other universities, but in the quality and number of those in orders I think few universities in Europe can equal it. It has today about ninety masters and doctors. The city has ten monasteries and five convents, and few in Spain can equal them. It has six hospitals, two of which, one for Spaniards and one for Indians, are excellent in every way. There are five or six parishes, not to mention other churches, of which there are many. There are three boarding schools, of which the first to be founded, that of San Martín, has about two hundred students. This is the principal school for the Spaniards of the kingdom, and there are eighty students of art, theology, and canon law. I pass over the nobility and the illustriousness of the gentlefolk, and the *cabildo* and city council, which are so important. I omit the great transactions of our merchants, despite the fact that this has been the emporium and center of all the Indies, as well as many other things that could be said about its greatness. From what I have read in the histories, I maintain that few cities in this world have grown so fast. But it is not my intention to write its history, or that of any other city. I simply want to say that if in the cities and towns under its immediate jurisdiction there is need of a remedy for idolatry, as we have already said, what must the other places be like?

Something was said of this in Chapter 9 and in confirmation thereof I will add a letter that I received today, February 9, from Luis de Teruel. It is similar to the letter quoted in the previous chapter. In brief, he says essentially this:

Now that I have seen with my own eyes what goes on here, the Indians of the Archbishopric of Lima, who have caused so much trouble, seem like so many saints for even though we have discovered many huacas and sorcerers among them, rare have been those with formal and express dealings with the Devil. Their offerings have been like mere grass and of little account. But here, My Father, there are many demons, *succubi* and *incubi*, and so commonplace is the Indians' traffic with them that few persons are any more frightened by them nowadays than they are of one another. A cleric has told me of the existence of some thirty-three of these spirits in one town, all of them with well-known names, without mentioning those he was unable to discover. And two fathers who set out on a mission not far from here something over six months ago found a quantity of them. Their usual practice is to sacrifice to the huacas children without blemish or stain, chosen from the town. And the fathers freed I know not how many who were to be sacrificed in the first festival. Two other fathers set out in another direction and wrote back that there are about a thousand huacas and household gods in every town, all of them crying for remedy. May Our Lord send it to them, etc.

The letter goes further, but this enough for my purpose, to confirm and repeat what has been said and to demonstrate the need for missions and visits everywhere. In the more remote areas the need will be even greater. Experience has shown us what there is in the Lima area. I will sum up a very long letter written some four days ago from a place sixteen leagues away. It is from fathers Rodrigo Dávila and Juan de Cuevas, who are accompanying Dr. Alonso Osorio. They describe what they are doing in the mission referred to in the previous chapter, and here is what they say:

We were able to conjecture the importance of this mission from the difficulties that we encountered at the start. Our usual procedure in the towns is to carry on daily talks, sermons, and catechisms with Christian teaching at night while the Miserere is sung to the accompaniment of the organ. This is to prepare the Indians to reveal their hidden idolatry. We have found it most important to win the good will of the leading Indian. Confession has been so frequent that they hardly left us time to eat, and after a mouthful we had to return to the confessional. The people did not wish to attend church without having confessed. Many have also taken communion and seemed quite ready for it. It has been the same in every town. Let me give some details. A man came from a distant place asking us to set him on the road to salvation. He said that among errors of which he had been undeceived and which he shared with the rest of his town was that when a priest was sinful he did not say a good mass nor consecrate properly. For this reason, many persons did not wish to hear him and for that reason he had not gone to church in some time. We can see from this how important a good example is, for it is true that *Qui scandalizaverit unum de pusillis istis, expedit, ut suspendatur molla asinaria, et demergatur in profundum maris.* While we were performing our duties Dr. Osorio was performing his, and with the experience, efficiency, and sagacity he possesses, he uncovered many huacas that had been hidden from other visitors.

He discovered the huaca Huancarquirca, which stood in the middle of a public square to guard it, and another called Chenacoto, for the increase of corn, and one called Llaucapa, to raise the corn. There was also an irrigation ditch called Sica, and the old Indian who guarded it allowed no one else to use the water, for he said

that the water in it had been granted to his grandparents and that to him alone, as their grandson, belonged the right to use it for his fields. This ditch was handed over to common use and the Indian was punished.

In the windows of a church we chanced to see clearly two wooden monkeys, and suspecting what the matter was, we discovered that they worshiped them as supports of the building and that they had a long fable about them. Not far from another town is a river, and the Indians who were with us said that sometimes the river reaches such a flood stage that it is impossible to cross it and it carries away all the bridges that are built. Thus, for a long time they had been obliged to go without hearing mass or seeing a priest. As we were leaving the place, we saw a great and beautiful narrows formed by two great crags that overhang the river, an ideal place for a bridge. And when we asked why no bridge had been built there, the Indians said they were afraid to build one there because the Devil lived in that spot, and if any Indian ventured there he would straightway die. They said they sometimes hear thunder and drums from there and so they were terrified to look upon the place they had been talking about. We dismounted at once and went there, taking the Indians with us. We set up a large cross which they had brought from town. We read a Gospel and made plans for a bridge so that the Indians and the priest might be able to cross whenever the river was in flood.

On a very high hill, in the town of San Francisco, a huaca and three malquis were found which had been kept hidden from Dr. Francisco de Avila.

In San Damián there was an abundance of confessions and Communions, but we learned that when they cleaned out the irrigation ditches some of the Indians celebrated a three-day festival in honor of Ucacamar, with an offering of llamas. For this they were punished.

In the town of Topicocha was discovered the huaca Huarihuacancha, which had been hidden from Dr. Avila; they worshiped this for the increase of their herds.

In the towns of San Bartolomé de Soclliacancha and Santiago de Tumna no superstition was found. In the latter town, the Indian whom we mentioned in the first chapter lies buried. In the village of San Hierónymo drastic steps had to be taken, for they were much given to drunkenness. Thirty crosses which Dr. Diego Ramírez

had ordered placed there on the site of thirty huacas had been removed. He ordered them replaced and discovered thirty malquis and an important huaca named Yaromarca. They had gone back to performing some of the festivals of their paganism. Whenever there was a frost, they would summon those persons who had been born feet first, those with a harelip, and all who were twins, and the sorcerer would upbraid them for the frost, saying that it had occurred because they had not fasted from salt and pepper. He then would require them to fast for ten days in the ordinary manner and to abstain from relations with their wives. They were also ordered to confess their sins privately, and for a penance they were to wash and to perform the other ceremonies of their confession.

There was an Indian woman in one town who, in despair because of her husband's cruelty, had thrown herself three times into a river and each time the current had cast her up on the bank. Seeing herself there and thinking that the water would not drown her, she wondered what to do, since she could not endure her evil life. Two other women who were passing by told her the fathers were coming soon, and so she took courage and told her story to them, and they made peace between her and her husband.

In San Juan de Matucama there were a number of confessions and five malquis were discovered and burned.

It seemed like Holy Week anywhere, because of the number of confessions in San Matheo de Huánchor. In this town most of the people were docile and good natured. Here one of the visitors discovered a huaca named Huanchorvilca, which was a large stone. Beneath it was the mummy of an Indian named Huánchor, with his two children. They worshiped this Indian because, according to them, the town had its origin in him. This was burned and the ashes thrown into the river. They also worshiped as a huaca a very tall stone standing in the middle of the river, because it was from there that the Inca had ordered his virgins thrown into the water when they had sinned with regard to chastity. They also worshiped for the good of the harvest another huaca named Huanchura.

In San Diego de Carampoma it was discovered by the evidence thereof that they offered sacrifices to the huaca Carampoma (all ancient town names are those of the principal huaca) which, because of its size could not be pulled down, but a cross had been placed on top of it. Outside the town was a chapel which looked peculiar to the visitor despite its name of Magdalena. He ordered it torn down, and four zaramamas were found inside.

In the house of a certain Indian of this town a stone and some sacrifices were found inside a chapel that he had built, and there was no way to make him tell the name of the stone nor why he had it. And so he has been condemned to the house of Santa Cruz where perhaps he will tell. It was also discovered that when an Indian dies in this town they carry to the church with the body the clothing that he wore, and if unable to throw it into the grave after him, they burn it. They also take the hair of the dead and sacrifice it a year later. They do the same thing with the hair of boys when they reach a certain age. Ten malquis were also found and burned.

In the mission at Casta some objects were found which had been hidden from their first visitor, Dr. Hernando de Avendaño. Among these were two huacas called husband and wife, Ananllauto and Quicanllauto, which were worshiped to keep the water supply from failing. Another was called Carvallacolla and kept for the harvest of the fields and of the potato crop. Still another was called Namocoya, and nearby an Indian named Namoc and his two children were buried. These were burned.

We heard a report that about a league from here was a famous huaca named Atahuanca, guarded by a famous sorcerer. The latter was taken into custody and the visitor sent him with some other persons to fetch the huaca. A little way outside town the people got careless and the sorcerer escaped. He hid himself so well that although more than sixty Indians looked everywhere for him they could not find him. It is believed that he threw himself into the river rather than reveal the huaca. At this the people of the town were so frightened and upset that even threats failed to move them. And one of the fathers, seeing this confusion, said that he would fetch the huaca. Three Spaniards and many Indians went with him. They set out by climbing a rocky hill fit only for vicuñas, and they reached a place that could not be climbed on horseback, so high and steep was the cliff. The father dismounted, and seizing the cross, which he intended to raise on the site of the huaca, he used it for a staff and ascended in this way for more than a quarter of a league. On seeing his example, the Indians took courage and climbed in good spirits, shouting as they went along with the father. In this way they came to the highest point, where they found a fine large chapel made of flagstones, and upon the stone that roofed the chapel was a stone three or four feet high to guard what was inside. After removing this and the other stones they found a medium-sized stone idol inside, anointed with paria*c* and the blood of guinea pigs and llamas. There were also eleven small flat stones used as plates for sacrifices. Two of these had also been anointed with blood like the huaca. All this we brought to town and burned in the public square. What was left was broken into pieces and thrown deep into the river more than a league from town without the Indians' knowledge. Thus it may be forgotten forever. During this journey a father came upon a lagoon along the road. In the middle of it was a stone figure more than two yards high which had been set up there. As he did not like the looks of it, he managed to get two Indians to talk about it. They told him it was a huaca named Quepacocha, whose purpose was to keep the lagoon from drying up. They used its water for their fields at the proper season. The visitor meanwhile found out the same thing in town. In another town in this mission were two huacas, one in the square on the wall of the church cemetery, and another in front of it. The Indians worshiped them as guardians of the town. These huacas were disposed of like all the rest and crosses were put in their place.

This and many other things are contained in the letter, and from it one can infer the critical need for missions, visits, and second visits among the Indians. The Lord Prince of Esquilache, viceroy of this kingdom, understood this, and, as noted in the first chapter, not content merely with donating the equipment at the beginning of the visit for the six fathers who generally go out on missions in this archbishopric, he ordered the necessary equipment of mules and such should be henceforth maintained to permit three fathers to set out on missions with the visitor. This equipment is to be maintained in the bishoprics of the kingdom that are within his jurisdiction, that is, Huamanga, Cuzco, Arequipa, Chuquiabo, Los Charcos, Santa Cruz, and Quito. For it has sometimes happened that a mission could not take place for lack of equipment. Now it will not only be possible but easy for missions to take place

c Vermilion powder.

and their continuance will be encouraged for some time. When the first visit in this archbishopric has been concluded, we will go to the bishopric of Trujillo, for up to now no Jesuit house has been established there, although they exist in all the rest of the Indian communities. This bishopric was separated from that of Lima a few years ago.

There is no lack of persons moved to serve the Lord, who wish to take part in this work and who think it a glorious thing to help with their offerings. Dr. Hernando de Avendaño, who is presently assigned to this cathedral as priest, because he has experienced missions and visits and because he believes it acceptable to God Our Father, gives an offering of 400 reales a year to defray the expenses of missions so that they may increase and be perpetuated. Likewise, Prebendiary Miguel de Bovadilla, with the same purpose and good will and the high opinion that he has of the service of the Lord in the missions, has given more than four thousand pesos and eight reales for expenses. Both of these men urged me not to publish these facts, desiring them to be known only to God Our Father, for the love they bear Him. But it seemed to me right for their donations to be known so that their opinion and esteem for the importance of missions may be known. This we shall see in the following chapter, which is the last one in this treatise.

CHAPTER TWENTY

Of the Importance of Missions

ONE THING leads to another and although I shall probably add nothing to what I have already said, since for my purpose I have no need to do so, still it may occur to the reader of this work that I praise my needles a lot considering how blunt their points are, as the saying goes. It may also be thought that I am blind compared with those whose sight is what it should be. And some may say, and not without foundation, that we appear to be elevating our own Society in this kingdom of Peru through missionary effort, and that we seem to wish people to think that we are the only ones who work profitably with the Indians and have zeal for their conversion. The truth is that the first to engage in this task, those to whom the beginnings of Christianity in Peru are owed, are the numerous monks of the orders of Saint Dominic, Saint Francis, and Saint Augustine and Our Lady of Mercy who, after the discovery of this new world, took their place in it in the year of Our Lord 1535. The last to come, when the work was already begun and established, were those of the Society of Jesus, thirty-three years later in the year 1568.

No one can deny that all the other orders have done more work among the Indians and still do more work among them than our Society. For in addition to the fact that in the principal cities and seats of a bishopric there are establishments and monasteries of these five orders, it is also true that the Indians everywhere have someone at hand to help them, preach to them, and hear their confessions. And as the Indians usually go where they like or where they find most satisfaction, love, and good will, each order has a brotherhood to go out and preach to them. Thus in Lima we hear every Sunday, in the same square and almost at the same time, the different orders preaching; this variety makes an agreeable consonance and an agreeable impression on the eyes and ears of God and men. Among their missions and curacies, the other four orders take charge of many Indian towns in all the bishoprics. But our Society, for the reasons discussed by Father Acosta in his book *De Procuranda salute Indorum,* does not generally have missions like the other orders. In these they cultivate and teach thousands of Indians continually, diligently, and with solicitude and to the profit of those under their care, as everyone knows.

On the other hand, those of our Society came from Europe at great cost, and through the liberality of His Majesty the

King, our sovereign, to share the bread of Christian teaching with the little ones who were asking for it. Each of these men may have had a greater object and a wider field for the talent or talents which the Lord has given him. But there were Indians here in whose behalf they might be employed, and even though they came from a loftier calling, having arrived here, they went to work, quite without the consolation the Lord gives to those who teach. The same thing can be said of many important persons who have joined the Society here. Our chief concern is to busy ourselves with the well-being and fortune of the Indians, and we look upon a knowledge of Indian languages as a very special and important matter. With us this talent is at the head of the list of those that are highly regarded, for we believe it to be one of the noblest of talents.

If this be true, and in our common opinion it most surely is, then our Society serves and profits the Indian simply by teaching and confessing quietly those who come to seek them out in our house. They also help the Indians of the Cercado, which is outside the wall of the city of Lima, for this area is in the charge of our Society. We also help the Indians in the town of Iulí, in the bishopric of Chuquiavo, where there are four notably ornamented parish churches, and these two posts or residences, as we call them, serve the many subjects living together with a superior as occurs in the boarding schools, one of which is a seminary for the Quechua language, and the other for Aymara, which are the two languages most in use in this kingdom. But if we had done these things without going out on missions, seeking out the Indians everywhere, the end and intention of our vocation would have been frustrated, and we would eat, as they say, our bread in vain.

Furthermore, there are many special duties incumbent upon the Society of Jesus, according to its statutes. Others are less incumbent upon it and in these it is surpassed by the other orders. The monks, for instance, by virtue of their vows, are inclined to the teaching of children and the uneducated. They keep school not only to teach grammar but also how to read and write. But our Society, in addition to other duties, has that of going on missions, as a matter most appropriate to its founding and specified as such in the bulls of its establishment. The custom of offering themselves for the purpose and standing ready to go wherever and however their superiors decide to send them seems so natural and proper to us that the contrary would seem alien and strange to the statutes of our Society. If for this reason the ecclesiastical and secular princes make more use of the members of our Society than they do of the members of other orders, it is not because they wish to show favor to some and disfavor to others, nor to show more confidence in some than in others, but because they wish to accommodate themselves to the vocation of each order. Thus they do not interrupt the normal course of events, and each order may serve the church and profit its neighbors in every way possible without breaking the statutes according to which they were called and chosen of God. As the ministry of missions is of such importance for our fellow men, as experience has shown, the superiors of the orders have not been content merely with having their members working in the curacies and mission stations and in other ministries concerned with the Indians but have offered to provide the secular and ecclesiastical authorities with men of religion well qualified to help in this task of extirpating idolatry. So, in effect, they have gone out with the visitors, as we have seen. Experience has also shown that for the moment to go out without visitors is inexpedient. Nor is it suitable for visitors to be numerous. Therefore, to help those who have gone out and are still going out, the princes have laid their hand on the fathers of our Society, considering them free and unhampered and obliged for so many reasons to perform this ministry, to serve the prelates, and to help carry the burden of many souls which the Lord has placed upon their shoulders.

Notwithstanding everything that has been said thus far, some religious have gone on missions alone among the Indians and, then as now, have achieved remarkable results. Such a man was Father Francisco or Friar Miguel Cano (for not everyone is agreed as to his name) of the Dominican order.

Of this friar several mentions have been made on the preceding pages. Similar a few years back was the case of Father Francisco de Mendoza, of the Franciscan order, of whom many edifying stories are told to the glory of the Lord Our God. Very recently Father Friar Gregorio de Bolívar and three other Franciscans have gone into the Andes in the region of Chuquiavo in the province of Chunchos, already referred to. The Indians have received them with a great show of contentment and the curaca, or king of the province, sent his own son with some Indians to Chuquiavo as hostages. The religious who were there sent for more religious to help them; the bishop of Chuquiavo wrote about this to the commissioner general. At about the same time, or a little before, Father Friar Joseph García Cabello and Father Friar Baltasar Buitrón of the order of Saint Augustine, with a companion whose name I have not been able to find out, came into the same province, and they also were admired *in captura piscium,* they sent for help. Four others have been designated by the same sacred order to go to their assistance. Two years ago Father Friar Melchor de Espinar, Father Friar Rodrigo Torices, a reader of theology, and Father Friar Domingo Gonçález came into the province of Los Motilones through Chechapoyas. Today they are alone among the Indians, who almost always refuse to let in Spanish soldiers. Yet they let in priests and monks when they want to come. Members of other orders have also gone out into other places, but of these I do not have a complete account.

Let us ask the Lord and Master of all wealth to send many of His workers with the spirit and zeal to increase and perfect the Christianity of the Indians, and to try, all else forgotten, to save their souls. With their eyes set upon what alone they should be set upon, that is, the glory of God, let them continue to serve and know and love those whom they did not love, nor serve, nor know. Nor let those whose good fortune it is to work in this enterprise hold for idle those who through obedience must remain in their cells or confessionals, pulpits, or cathedra, or choir. For they, from wherever they are, are accustomed to help more with their prayers in this spiritual battle against the Devil than those even who go into it with weapons in their hands, for thus did Moses in the fighting of his nation against the Amaleks. And let not those who stay, as it were, in shade and repose, judge the intentions of those who go out into the sun and busy themselves with ministries in which there are so many causes and occasions of distraction as there are in missions. For if the religious do what we believe they ought to do, if they would seem religious, they will display to the highest degree the most excellent of virtues. No one who goes on a mission, unless his faith is fervent and alive, is able to enliven what is cold, lukewarm, or dead in those who should confess, catechize, and preach. From a cold or lukewarm breast no fervent or lively words will come, nor will there be the hope and confidence in God which conquers great difficulties, meets many obstacles, and suffers the spiritual and the physical impediments which occur each day. Nor can they fight against them nor persevere long in them. *Nisi charitas Christi urgeat nos.* The love of God is most needful, and an esteem for the souls redeemed by His blood in order to tax the mind day after day with catechizing and confessing rude folk, poor sick people, and deaf old people, repeating the same thing a thousand times until they hear it and get some idea of it. Humility and patience will not fail to increase in the midst of numerous and never-ending acts of virtue. For ministry among the Indians does not bring the pleasure nor the popular applause that is so frequently sought by Spaniards. What courage is required to keep from fainting or falling or being frightened by the impediments raised by the Devil! He wishes to keep himself from being deprived of a possession that he had tyrannized for so many years. What prudence is needed to foresee events and to bring others to pass, to satisfy those who do not believe that evil exists, to answer those who doubt and oppose those who do not believe that evil exists, to answer those who doubt and oppose those who contradict, especially if they are learned, pious, and powerful persons!

Although we do not seek out hardships, we will have more

frequent occasions to exercise self-control than to rejoice at
the rough roads, the tumble-down churches, and uncomfortable
living quarters, and when the missionaries return to their
mission house, they will think the poorest and least com-
fortable place in it a delight. What shall I add concerning the
trials of chastity, the acts of poverty and necessity, of the time
and material available for silent prayer and for familiar dealings with the Lord Our God, and the occasions to exercise the
other virtues? For it may well be feared that he who does not
return from his mission with an increase in the qualities he
took with him will have left little profit to his neighbors. And
those who by the grace of Our Lord God who have truly
experienced it within themselves will be able to say: *Euntes
ibant et flebant mittentes semina sua venientes autem venient
cum exultatione portantes manipulos suos.* Truly will they be
His when they have piled sheaves into the granary and looked
more to their spiritual well-being than to that of others, for
*charitas bene ordinata incipit a se ipsa et quid prodest homini,
si universum mundum lucretur animae vero suae detrimentum
patiatur.* It would plainly be foolish not to assure the life of
the soul of those who endure so many risks and dangers to
the body, for five or six fathers have died while on missions
within the last few years.

I conclude this whole treatise, therefore, by saying that all
that is said in it is yet less than what might have been said.
For it is one thing to see and touch something with the hands
and another merely to hear about it. Because there is no one
who sees this enterprise, if he possesses any zeal for the glory
of God and esteem for the souls which cost so much toil,
who would not wish to have a thousand lives to employ them
all in this enterprise. And so, I beg and I urge those of you
who read this to pray and supplicate earnestly the Lord Our
God to pity the people who are so unprotected, to move the
hearts of those who ought to be moved, to provide a remedy
and provide the means and the wherewithal which the
seriousness of this great evil demands.

Finis

An Edict against Idolatry

I, ———, visitor general and ecclesiastical judge of this archbishopric in the cases of idolatry, in the name of the illustrious ——— of His Majesty's Council, bring greetings and grace to you, our neighbors, the dwellers in and inhabitants of this town. You know and are to know that the holy fathers, illuminated by the Holy Spirit, in sacred and holy councils, have justly and properly ordained that all prelates and pastors of the church (unless they are legitimately prevented) are each of them obliged to make a general visitation and solemn scrutiny of the life and customs of all subjects every year, which was appropriate for the profit and spiritual well-being of souls. And since their salvation consists in their being in grace and charity and far away from and separated from their sins, and especially those of idolatry by which they deny the worship of the one true God and give it to His creatures, wherefore, for the discharge of conscience and as pertaining to the spiritual health and well-being of your souls, we exhort and command that if any of you know of anything relating to what is manifest before me within the three days, which I allot to you and point out as a time limit, the last of which will be peremptory according to law, having it dearly understood that when the aforesaid time limit has elapsed we will proceed against those who are rebellious with all the vigor of the laws.

1. Whether you know of any person or persons, men or women, who have worshiped or adored huacas, hills, or springs, asking them for health, life, and worldly goods.

2. Item. Whether you know of any person or persons who have worshiped the sun, moon, or the stars they call Oncoy, which are the Pleiades, or the stars they call chacras, which are the three Marys, or the morning star which they call Pachahuárac or Coyahuárac.

3. Item. Whether you know any person or persons who

have worshiped the huaca called *cónpac* at the time when the irrigation ditches are cleaned out for the sowing, or the huacas called huanca or chíchic, which they have on their farms and to which they offer sacrifices of chicha, coca, burned tallow, and other things.

4. Item. Whether you know any person or persons who have in their houses huacas, household gods called conopas or zaramamas for the increase of their corn, or caullamas for the increase of their herds, or divining stones[a] called *ylla*, which they worship for the aforementioned effect, and with which they have mullu, paria, llacsa, asto, sancu, and other offerings which are given.

5. Item. Whether you know any person or persons who worship lightning, calling it Líbiac, and saying that it is the lord and creator of the rain, and offer it sacrifices of llamas, guinea pigs, and other things.

6. Item. Whether you know any person or persons who worship their pacarinas and the mummies and bones of their pagan ancestors which they call malquis, and the mummies and bones of huaris, making offerings and sacrifices to them.

7. Item. Whether you know of any person or persons who, when they go on the road, throw down at the top of a hill big hollow stones, chewed coca, chewed corn, or anything else by spitting, asking them to take away their weariness on the road.

8. Item. Whether you know any Indian or Indians in this town who are witches or charmers or have a pact with the Devil.

9. Item. Whether you know of any person or persons who celebrate the festivals of the huacas, offering them sacrifices or offerings of llamas, guinea pigs, mullu, paria, llacsa, burned tallow, sancu, parpa, coca, and other things.

10. Item. Whether you know of any person or persons who fast during the festivals of their huacas, not eating salt or pepper for some days, abstaining from sleeping with their lawful wives for this ceremony, and washing themselves in the

[a] *Piedras bezares. Supra,* p. 146, n. *b.*

streams, believing that with this washing their sins are forgiven.

11. Item. Whether you know any Indians who confess their sins to sorcerers or ministers of idolatry during the festivals of the huacas. Or whether, when they are ill or afflicted by sorrow, the aforesaid sorcerers rub their heads with a little stone called pasca, or with ground corn, or whether, killing a guinea pig, they see in the blood of the entrails signs with which to tell the future.

12. Item. Whether during the aforementioned festivals of the huacas you know of their staying up all night singing, drinking, and dancing the pagan ceremony of the pacarícuc.

13. Item. Whether you know that when they get their crops they perform a ceremony and a dance called the ayrigua, tying ears of corn to a stick or branch and dancing with them, or another dance they call *ayja* or *quaucu,* playing an instrument called the succha,[b] or any other kind of dance accompanied with pagan ceremonials and superstitions.

14. Item. Whether you know of any person or persons who cut their children's hair, calling it huarca or pacto, and performing certain ceremonies to which they invite their sons-in-law, whom they call masa, or their uncles, whom they call caca, drinking, singing, and dancing, and giving the aforesaid children names different from those given in baptism.

15. Item. Whether you know of any person or persons who say that the souls of the dead go to Huarochaca or Upaimarca rather than to Hell, Heaven, or Purgatory. And when a person dies, whether on the fifth day they give food and drink to the dead man's soul by burning corn and pouring out chicha.

16. Item. Whether you know of any person or persons who have disinterred the bodies of dead Christians from the churches, stealing them and taking them to the burial places called machays, where their malquis are.

17. Item. Whether you know that when the Indians go to do forced labor on their farms, in the fields, or any other work, they urge the sorcerers to pray to the huacas for them. And

[b] *Supra,* p. 50, n. *d.*

when they are in the *yunga*,^c whether they worship the sea, pulling out eyelashes and eyebrows.

18. Item. Whether you know of a woman who has given birth to twins, which they call chuchu, or a child born feet first, which they call chacpa. Whether the woman in question fasts certain days according to pagan ceremony, not eating salt or pepper, nor sleeping with her husband, shutting herself up in a secret place where she cannot be seen, and whether, if one of the children dies, they keep it in a jar for a pagan ceremony.

19. Item. Whether you know of any person or persons already grown up and of an age to be baptized, or already baptized, who are called by the name of their huaca, or by that of thunder, calling themselves Curi, or of the lightning, Líbiac.

20. Item. Whether you know of huacas that have property dedicated to their worship such as gold, silver, copper, clothing made of cumbi, vessels of silver, huamas, *hincas*, tincurpas, llamas, chacras, and other things.

21. Item. Whether you know of any Indian who for a pagan rite wears huarás secretly beneath their drawers, or without them.

22. Item. Whether you know of any person or persons who have said that all men do not have their origin in Adam and Eve, but that each clan has a different pacarina from which it comes.

23. Item. Whether you know of any person or persons who, when they gather the corn, keep the ears they call *huantas*, *airigua*, *micsazara*, *mamazara*, or *collauzara* for a pagan ceremony in which they are burned and offered to the huacas.

Anyone who knows about any of these things or has heard of such things, as declared above, must denounce them and make them known before me within the aforesaid three days. Those who act contrary to this and are rebellious will be punished with all the rigor of the law. Given, etc. . . .

^c Lowlands.

Regulations to Be Left by the Visitor in the Towns
as a Remedy for the Extirpation of Idolatry

IN THE TOWN of ————, on the ———— day of the month of ————, 16——, ————, visitor general and ecclesiastical judge of the archbishopric in the cases of idolatry, for His Illustrious Lordship ————, having completed the visit conducted in this town concerning the aforesaid idolatry, in order to remove from it every occasion for a relapse, and so that the offense to Our Lord God may cease, by the commission he holds from His Most Illustrious Lordship ————, has drawn up and ordained the following regulations.

First. If from now on any Indian man or woman shall lapse into idolatry, worshiping huacas, hills, streams, lightning, the sun, moon or stars, or perform any of the ancient ceremonies of his paganism, the priest or vicar of the mission shall write down the case, substantiating it, and remitting it to His Illustrious Lordship ————, or to his provisor, together with the name of the guilty so that they may be sentenced, and it is advisable that His Lordship should know of any lapses that occur so that he may provide a suitable remedy. And if the relapsed person is a sorcerer or minister of idolatry, this regulation will be applied with greater force.

Item. From now on no Indian, man or woman, shall be called by the name of a huaca or by the name of lightning. Therefore, he may not be named Curi, Manco, Missa, Chacpa, Líbiac, nor Santiago, but Diego instead; and if anyone gives any of these names to his child, he will be given one hundred lashes through the streets, and the priest or vicar shall proceed against him as one relapsed into idolatry. And those who up to now have been called by any of the aforesaid names, I now order to cease and desist and to accommodate themselves to being called by other surnames, that is Spanish names or saints' names.

Item. The priest holding the benefice of a town will take

particular pains to prevent the celebrations that the Indians observe at seed time, when they indulge in drinking and singing, which continue to be a great offense to the Lord Our God, etc. He will make every effort to see to it that when they send out the aforesaid invitations, the celebrants are given something to eat but prevented from drinking excessively as has been done up to now.

Item. From now on in no case nor for any reason will the Indians of this town, whether men or women, play drums, dance, or sing and dance at a marriage or town festival, singing in their mother tongue as they have done up to now. For experience has shown that in these songs they invoke the names of their huacas, the malquis, and the lightning, which they worship. And any Indian who breaks this rule will be given one hundred lashes and have his hair cut, and his crime will be proclaimed publicly. If a cacique dances or sings, as herein described, the curate or vicar of the town will write a report and send it, accompanied by the aforesaid guilty cacique to the Illustrious Lord Archbishop, or his provisor, so that he may be punished.

Item. The priest of this town will strictly enforce the decrees against drunkenness and chicha made of *jora* which the most excellent of kings has promulgated, for this is the most efficacious means of destroying idolatry and wiping out the drunkenness of the caciques as well as that of the rest of the Indians. Extreme rigor and every means of punishment should be used in addition to preaching and teaching, prohibiting them from assembling publicly or secretly to get drunk during their festivals, or during the Christmas and Easter seasons, or during the festivals of the advocation of the town, and every Indian who does so should be punished severely and upon the caciques should be executed the penalties laid down in the aforesaid decrees for the improvement of their ways. And let the rest of the Indians follow their good example.

Item. From now on Indian sorcerers and ministers of idolatry must not cure the sick in any way, because experience has shown that when they effect cures they cause those who are sick to become idolaters and to confess their sins to them in the pagan manner. And if there be any other Indians who know how to effect cures, because they are acquainted with the properties of herbs, the local priest will make sure that the manner of the cure is free from superstition.

Item. From now on no Indian of either sex will keep mullu, paria, or llacsa, or will make a sancu or tecti, nor will he have an asto, nor keep the corn they call *huantay*, airigua, micsazara or collauzara, nor will they keep with potatoes, *ocas*,[a] *camotes*,[b] or *yucas*,[c] and anyone who breaks this rule will be given one hundred lashes and his hair shorn, and proceedings will be started against him for having lapsed into idolatry.

Item. When they take in the crops they will not dance the dance called ayrihua, which is performed by fastening ears of corn to a stick and dancing with them, nor the dance called ayja, or huanca, nor will they play succhas, and anyone who breaks this rule will be given one hundred lashes and will be held one week in jail.

Item. From now on the Indians, male and female, of this town will not fast as they used to in the pagan manner, eating neither salt nor pepper, and if anyone breaks this rule he will have proceedings started against him as one lapsed into idolatry. And the priest and vicar of the town will start proceedings against those who break this rule, as against persons lapsed into idolatry.

Item. From now on the Indians of this town will not place cooked or roasted food upon the tombs of the dead, for it is a common error of the Indians, practiced up to now, to believe that the souls of the dead eat and drink. The priests of the town will take particular care to see to it that the doors of the church are always kept well locked and guarded and that the keys are kept by a trustworthy person, because experience has shown that they often dig up Christian bodies from the

[a] A tuber like the potato.
[b] A sweet potato.
[c] *Yucca.* The common yard plant, whose roots when cooked taste something like a potato.

churches and take them to the burial places of their pagan ancestors. Anyone who breaks this rule will have proceedings started against him as one lapsed into idolatry.

Item. From now on, no Indian, man or woman, will clip the hair of the children, which they call huarca, with the ceremonies performed heretofore, and an Indian who has sons or daughters with a full head of hair will present them to the priest of the town before having their hair cut, so that he can send them to a servant of his who will cut it, thus preventing the aforesaid ceremonies. Anyone who breaks this rule will be given one hundred lashes.

Item. The sorcerers, male and female, and ministers of idolatry who have been listed in the book of the church and on the tablet that is hanging on the wall, will be gathered together morning and afternoon for Christian teaching, as the children are, and whoever stays away without the priest's permission will be given twelve lashes, and if he repeats the offense, he will be punished with greater rigor.

Item. Henceforth a festival of the Holy Cross will be held every year on the day of its exaltation, on the fourteenth of September, in memory of the triumph over idolatry obtained by its means. During this festival a mass will be sung and the holy cross will lead the procession and the priest of the mission will preach to the Indians, telling why the festival is being celebrated and exhorting them to give thanks to the Lord for having lifted them out of their errors. And the Indians will give to the priest of the mission and town three pesos as alms for the mass and sermon. And the majordomos of the church will beg alms from door to door with a cross, making it plain to the Indians that the alms are voluntary and that what is collected by this means will be listed in the book of the church and used to buy candles for the aforesaid festival.

Item. The priest and vicar of this mission must be advised that all the Indians of his mission worshiped huacas, conopas, huancas, or chíchic, the sun, moon and stars, and especially the Pleiades, which they call Oncoy, and the three Marys,

which they call chacra, or the thunder and lightning; that
they had in their house idols or household gods called conopas;
that they worshiped their ancestors, whom they called malquis,
as well as huaris and pacarinas; that they used to celebrate a
festival every year to the aforesaid huacas with the sacrifice
of llamas and guinea pigs and offerings of chicha, mullu, paria,
llacsa, sancu, coca, and burned tallow; that they fasted on
certain days, not eating salt or pepper and abstaining from
sleeping with their wives; that their sorcerers and ministers
of idolatry received the confession of their sins in the pagan
manner and that the aforesaid sorcerers were accustomed to
preach at their festivals, telling them that the God of the
Spaniards was for Spaniards only, whereas the huacas were
for the Indians; that their progenitors came from their
pacarinas, for which reason they deny the origin of all men
in Adam and Eve and say that there is a place appointed
where the souls go called Upaimarca, where the souls eat and
drink. For these reasons it is important for the priest of this
mission to take special pains in his preaching. He should
refute their errors and teach them the true way of salvation
so that the Indians may know Christ, Our Redeemer, for if
they do not do so, the Lord Our God will demand of them a
strict accounting of the flock which they have in their care.
And this was to be signed.

*These rules may be added to, subtracted from, or changed
in whatever way seems expedient.*

APPENDIX

Quechua Glossary

IN THE COURSE of his book Father Arriaga used more than two hundred Quechua words. Of these he thought it necessary to provide a Spanish meaning for no more than sixty-four. Usually this matters little, for he nearly always provided parenthetical translations of Quechua words. At other times he seems to have assumed that a word once defined needs no further definition. Still other words he never defined at all, although from the context the meaning is generally clear. Of the several Quechua dictionaries available the translator owes most to that of Jorge Lira (*Diccionario kkechuwa-español*, Instituto de Historia, Lingüística y Folklore, publicaciones especiales, 12, Universidad nacional de Tucumán, Tucumán, Argentine Republic, 1945).

A curious fact about Father Arriaga is that his colleague Father Dávila says that he did not know the Indian language. This is difficult to believe, for not only does he make extensive use of individual words but also quotes some long phrases. Further, in no case did the translator find his interpretation in error when checked against modern dictionary entries. And as the reader will have noted he lays great stress on the importance of knowing the native language if one would work effectively with the Indians.

On the following pages the words included in Father Arriaga's glossary are indicated by an asterisk. Most of the definitions have been supplied from the text itself. When another source had to be used, the fact is indicated by enclosing the definition in brackets.

Father Arriaga, an indifferent speller in Spanish at times, frequently is guilty of more than one spelling of Quechua words. These variant spellings have been left in the English text but are included in the glossary with cross references.

Finally, the glossary is just that, an index to the Quechua words in the text. To deal with all the problems raised by the Indian language as used in a text even as short as this one would require more space than is available. There are many excellent books available for those who would pursue the subject further. The aim here is simply to provide a guide to the English text of Father Arriaga's Spanish treatise.

The transliteration of Quechua words and place names that appear in Father Arriaga's earliest printed text is not always reflected by his latest Peruvian editor, Mr. Urteaga. Except in cases where the latter has corrected an obvious mistake in the first edition, the translator has respected Father Arriaga's spelling. Consonantal *i* and *u* have been replaced by *j* and *v* according to modern usage.

acataymita.   festival for the ripening of avocados

acca (asua, azua).   chicha, a wine or beer made of corn or other ingredients; *see also* tecti

accac (açuac, azuac).   chicha maker

acequia (azequia).   ditches for the service of the house; [irrigation ditches]

açuac.   *see* accac

*agí (ají).   hot pepper of the Indians

*aillo (ayllo).   faction or lineage; [clan]

*aillo.   three-branched cord with a lead ball at each end, used to hunt birds or animals by entangling them [commonly known by the Argentine name of *bolas*]

airigua (ayrigua).   kind of corn; a dance done with corn stalks to celebrate the festival of the corn harvest

ají.   *see* agí

ambicamayo.   healer

anaco.   lady's mantle or cape

antari.   coiled horns

apachita.   heap of stones piled up by weary travelers

*aquilla.   drinking vessel

asto (ato).   plumes; bird from which plumes are procured

astop tuctu.   red plumes from the huacamaya bird or other bird of the Andes

asua.   *see* acca

ato. *see* asto

aucachic. confessor; *see also* ichuri

auqui (auquilla). sorcerer who kills with his witchcraft

auquilla. *see* auqui

aut. small fruit that is dry, similar to espingo

axaconopa. potato totem or object sacred to potatoes

axomama. mother potato; first potato; double potato

ayja. dance

ayllo. *see* aillo, first meaning

ayri. corn; ear of corn

ayrihua. *see* airigua

ayrihuaimita. festival of the harvest of corn

ayrihuayzara. double ear of corn; doll to protect the corn and ensure a good crop

*azequia. *see* acequia

azua. *see* acca

azuac. *see* accac

binço. very fine blue powder

*bira. tallow; grease; llama fat

*biracocha (viracocha). sea foam; a name applied to the Spaniards; the creator god

*caca. maternal uncle

cacahuachi. ceremony consisting of throwing sticks into a hole

callpacta ricusum. divining by means of guinea pig entrails

cámac. the creator

*camachico. an Indian who has the duty of calling people together, or bearing a message; ruler of the clan

caman. talent; skill; cleverness; by extension, foresight; knowledge of the future or of a secret

camasca. doctor; one who divines by means of kernels of corn

camayoc llama. charm for the increase of the herd

*camiseta. sleeveless Indian garment [actually Spanish, not Quechua]

camote. sweet potato

carua. word unknown to the glossaries, perhaps equivalent to a human figure or doll

caruayquispina. person of whom the Indians are afraid; rite of burning a soul by burning a figurine made out of fat

carvamuqui. yellow powders

caucho. kind of witch; appellation in the chinchasuyo of the clever, intelligent, diligent man caulla.   bitter

caullama.   shortened form of camayoc llama

caullazara.   bright-colored ears of corn kept for their magical properties

cayan.   places from which huacas are invoked

*chácara (chacra).   farm; farmhouse

chacha.   sorcerer

chachi.   female child born feet first

*chacpa.   child born feet first

chacra.   *see* chácara

chacrahinca.   half-moon of silver

chacrayoc.   large stone placed on a house to protect it

chanca.   household god

chaquira.   a bead of colored glass

checan.   that is true

*chicha.   wine or beer made of corn or other ingredients

chíchic.   large stone placed on a house to protect it

chinchasuyu.   north

*choclo.   the ear or head of grain of maize, which is the Indians' wheat when it is dry

*chuchu.   when two are born of one belly; fruit or corn growing double

*chumbi.   woman's sash

chunpirum.   bagful of small stones for divining

*chuspa.   purse or pocket; cloak

*coca.   a shrub whose thin leaves the Indians chew, and they carry them in the mouth without swallowing them; this used to be one of the great sources of profit in Peru

cocamama.   totem for the increase of coca

collasuyu.   south

collauzara.   kind of ear of corn

compa.   stone placed in the irrigation ditch to protect it

*condor.   vulture but twice as big as those in Spain

conopa.   small sacred object owned and worshiped privately

conpac.   ceremony of cleaning out the irrigation ditches before sowing

contisuyu.   west

*criollo.   Spaniard born over here

*cui (cuy).   guinea pig

*cumbi.   cloth or clothing; fine, delicate, dainty

*curaca. head or principal man among the Indians
curi. when two are born of one belly
*cuy. *see* cui
cuyaspa. for the love they bear
cuyrícuc. divining by means of guinea pig entrails
cuzco. navel; center
espingo. tree indigenous to Peru; a dry fruit like a round almond, very bright in color, although not very good
guanaco. a cameloid smaller than the llama
hacarícuc. divining by means of guinea pig entrails
hayrihuasara (huayriguazara). two kernels of white and black corn growing out together; two ears of corn
*hicho (ichu). a grass like Spanish grass but finer (which grows on the high plateaus)
hillapa. lightning
hinca. half moon of silver
*huaca. idol or place of worship; a sacred object; also taken in the sense of treasure
huacahuanrimac (huacahuarmac). one who talks with a huaca
huacamaya. plumes of various colors
huacanquis. love potion
huacapvillac. one who talks to the huaca
huachi. straight sticks; divining by throwing straight sticks at an opening
huachua. white plumes of birds of the same name found in the lagoons of the high plateaus
huacicamayoc. majordomo; porter; keeper of the house
huacon. dance of the festival of Oncoy
huacra. necklace or high collar of various colors
huahua. white feathers
*huama. crown something like a diadem for the head; falcon or totem
*huanca. fertilizer for the land
huanca. large stone placed on a house to protect it
huantay. tall ear of corn
huantayzara. tallest corn, high on the stalk; doll supposed to protect the corn
*huaraca. very thin cord worn around the head; slingshot
huaráclla. spirits
huarás. breechclout

huarca. hair that is cut off and kept

huari. native to a town without any recollection of having come from outside; first dwellers of the land

huarochacha. place where the dead souls go

huasicama. majordomo; porter; keeper of the house

huassa. a stone swaddled like an infant

huata. year

huatana. place where an animal is tied for sacrifice

huatcuna. ceremony performed with silver or when powders or eyelashes are blown toward the huaca

*huayco. defile; deep valley

huaylli. song; dancing song

huayriguazara (huayrihuasara). two grains of black and white corn growing together; two ears from one stalk

hucllachacuininta. communion or gathering of the saints

humara. sleeveless shirt

humu macsu (humu maxa). privileged male born feet first

humu maxa. see humu macsu

ichu. a grass like Spanish grass but finer (which grows on the high plateaus)

ichuri. confessor; one who gathers straw

illapa. arquebus called lightning

*inca. common name of the ancient kings of Peru

inti. the sun

intiphuatana. place where the victim of the sun is tied

intisuyu. east

jora (sora, zara, zora). kind of corn used in making chicha

laca. small pointed or angular stone crystals regarded as totems

*ladino. sly, clever [Spanish, not Quechua]

laicca. sorcerer who kills with his witchcraft

*lampa. spade or shovel with which the Indians dig

larca villana. stone or totem placed in an irrigation ditch

líbiac (llíbiac). lightning; god of lightning

libiacvíllac. one who speaks to lightning

*libis. three-branched cord with a lead ball at each end, used to hunt birds or animals by entangling them [commonly known by the Argentine name of bolas]

llacsa. green color in the form of either powder or stone, like copper oxide

llacta. city

llactacamayoc (llactayoc). governor of the people

llactayoc. *see* llactacamayoc

llacuaz. person whose ancestors moved to a town from elsewhere

*llama. sheep of the land, though more resembling a camel, of the size of a medium-sized calf. The Indians have no other beast of burden than this one. It will carry about half as much as ours.

llamapcamayoc. totem for the increase of the herd

llampis. cup or vessel

llíbiac. *see* líbiac

llicla (lliclla). shawl

lluviac. a huaca that is worshiped to cause rain

*maçamorra (mazamora). porridge or gruel [made of corn]

machay. burial place of ancestors

macsa. one who effects cures with tricks or superstitions

*maiz. wheat of the Indians [maize, corn]

malquipvíllac. one who talks to the malquis

malquis. mummy of an Indian ancestor; a plant

mamacocha. sea

mamapacha. earth; mother earth

mamazara. mother of the corn; ears of an unusual shape, or several joined together

manapac. sorcerer

manchucu. love potion

*manta. square Indian cape [Spanish, not Quechua]

mantur. red color

*marca aparac (marcaparac). head man or representative of a town (region)

marcachara (marcayoc). head man or representative of a town

marcaparac. *see* marca aparac

*masa (massa). son-in-law or close relative

matayzara. bright-colored ears of corn kept for their magical properties

*mate. plate made of something like a squash which looks as if God had made it for no other purpose

mayuchulla. ceremony of drinking water before crossing a stream

mazamora. *see* macamorra

michacasara. first corn that ripened; brightly colored ears of corn

micui (micuy). meal; to eat

micuy. *see* micui

minga. a gathering to build a house
*mingar. to invite or hire someone with pay to do something
*mita. an order or an occasion for doing something
*mochar. to worship or reverence
mólcoc. that which renews or rejuvenates
mollo (mullu). large seashell; [small pieces thereof]
morpis. household god
moscoc. divination through dreams
*mullu. *see* mollo
munaos. mummies of Indian ancestors
muscuc. dreamer
muscuy. dream
*naturales. Indians [not Quechua]
ñaca. hair that is cut off
oca. tuber like the potato
oncoy. the Pleiades; seven goats
oroso. species of spider
p. genitive particle corresponding to *of* or *of the*
pacaric. what is reborn; what returns; the dawn
*pacarícuc. all-night vigil accompanied by dancing, drinking, and
    singing
pacarina. place where the Indians say they have their origin
paccha. species of spider
pachácac. majordomo of the huacas
pachacaricuc (pachacatic, pachacuc). foretelling the future by
    means of spiders
pachca. spider
pacho. corn or sweet corn
pacto. hair that is cut off; equal bodies or those similar in form or
    color
*palla. important or leading lady
*papa. root commonly eaten by the Indians; [potato]
papaconopa. a potato totem or object sacred to potatoes
paria. vermilion powders
pariana. elected minister who guards the fields
parihuana (pariuna). rose-colored plumes like those of the
    bird of the same name
pariuna. *see* parihuana
parpa. a ball or mass of corn mixed with salt and used for
    sacrifices

pasca. little stone meaning pardon

pichga (pisga, pishga). five; game played with little striped sticks

*pincollo. bone or cane flute

piripiri. amulet or philter to cause love

*pirua. storehouse for corn

piruazara. ears of corn whose rows of kernels are not in a straight line but in a spiral like a snail shell

pisga. *see* pichga

pishga. *see* pichga

pucllachacuininta. jest or merriment of the saints

*puna. cold, mountain area; [high plateau]

punchao (punchau). the sun in its daytime aspect; lord of the day

punchau. *see* punchao

punchaupvíllac. one who talks to the sun; priest of the sun

*puquio. streams and springs

pututu. bone flute

qqespina. guard; remedy; defense; by extension, refuge

quaucu. dance

*quepa. trumpet

quero. inca drinking vessel

quicu. conopa consisting of a sharp stone

quilcasca chaque. painted lance

quilla. moon

quillahuañun. the moon dies

quillatutayan. the moon grows dark

*quinua. small white seed cooked like lentils; [an Andean grain grown at high altitudes]

quipo (quipu). an Indian mnemonic device consisting of knotted cords

quipocamayo. keeper of the records

quipu. *see* quipo

rao. snow

rapyac. sorcerer or witch

razu. snow-covered mountains

ripiac. diviner who moves the fleshy parts of his arms

ritri. snow

ropyac (rapyac). sorcerer or witch

runa. man

runa camac (runapcamac). creator of man

runapcamac. *see* runa camac
runapmicuc. man-eater
sacyac (socyac). foretelling the future by means of corn
sanacoyoc. doctor
sancu (sango). ball of corn meal
sango. *see* sancu
sarachuchu. double or twin ears of corn
sipastarina. a proof that one is loved by throwing sticks at an opening "in order to sleep with a woman"
socyac. *see* sacyac
soncoy. heart
soncoyac. doctor
sora. *see* jora
succha. instrument made from the skull of the guanaco
*taclla. hoe; plow peculiar to the Indians
tambo. relay or rest stop on Inca messenger routes
tamta. kind of ruff
taqui huahua. twins
taquies. carousing
*taripados. those who have been examined
*taripar. to examine
taruca (taruga). animal of these parts, similar to the mountain goat
*taruga. *see* taruca
*tecti. a thick chicha or wine
tincuna. where two rivers come together
*tincunacuspa. sexual relations before marriage
tincurpa. little round medal or clasp; ceremony in which an Indian's head is rubbed with a stone and he is washed with corn meal and water
tocanca. ceremony consisting of spitting on a stone during a wearisome journey
*topo. clasps like long pins, but with a large head, and flat like the palm of the hand
tuctu. plume or something that sprouts
tumi. sea lions
*ujuta. Indian sandal or shoe
umu. sorcerer
Upamarca (Upaimarca). silent land or land of the dumb (i.e. the dead)

viccaryaycu. [climbing up where one should not]

víllac. priest; those who cure with a thousand tricks

viracocha. *see* biracocha

yale. chicha offered to the huacas

yana. employee of an inferior occupation

yanacuna. lowly people

yanápac. minister's helper

ylla. stones [hair balls] found in the stomachs of animals and regarded as having magical properties

yucca. the common yard plant whose roots when cooked taste something like a potato

yunga. lowlands

zamana. places where the huacas rested or were located

zamarcan. rest in peace

zamay. tomb of rest

zara. *see* jora

zara conopa. corn totem

zaramama. mother of the corn

zora. *see* jora

INDEX

Acosta, Father Joseph, author of *De Procurando salute indorum,* 72, 135, 159

Acuña, Dr. Alberto de, judge of royal audience of Lima, 16, 144

Alvarez de Paz, Father Diego, 5

Ambar, province, witches found in, 40

Andahuaylas, town, sorceress found in, 40

Andajes, town, 18

Antolínez, Don Plácido de, priest holding special archepiscopal commission, 21

Arequipa, city, bishopric of, 77, 157

Arroyo, Father Benito de, visits Chichacochas and Tarma, 14

Avellenada, Don Hierónymo de, organizes execution, 12

Avendaño, Hernando de, serves mission of San Pedro de Casta, 15; vicar of Collana de Lampos, 17; findings of in mountains and lowlands, 20; burns huaca Huayna Xillin, 89; mentioned, 5, 6, 18, 37, 43, 75, 140, 141, 156, 158

Avila, Dr. Francisco de, priest of San Damián, first to deduce presence of hidden idolatry, 10; mentioned, 11, 12, 13, 14, 17, 18, 37, 43, 53, 70, 75, 154

Aymaráes, province, 77

Ayrauac, ruins of, huacas removed from, 89

Barranca, river, 51

Bolívar, Father Gregorio de, Franciscan friar, 162

Borja, Don Francisco de, patron of prince's school, 141

Bovadilla, Prebendary Miguel de, 158

Buitrón, Father Friar Baltasar, Augustinian friar, 162

Cacho de Santillana, Licentiate, 6

Cahacay, town, 81, 84, 86, 87

Cahuana, town in province of Conchucos, famous idol found in, 27; mentioned, 26

Cajatambo, corregidor district and province, 20, 53, 80

Cano, Miguel or Francisco. *See* Francisco

Carapachas Indians, in archbishopric of Huamalíes, 147

Casta, mission at, 156

Chachapoyas, town, espingo brought from, 4; mentioned, 148, 162

Chanca, town, 83

Chancay, corregidor district, 17, 20

Charcos (los), town, 78, 99, 157

Chaupiguaringas, town near Huánuco, 17

Chayna, town, 89

Chechapoyas (Chachapoyas), province, 162

Checras (Chacras), Dr. Avendaño priest in, 15; mentioned, 90, 139

children, bodies of returned to churches, 20; bodies of burned, 31; unusual birth of regarded as ill omen, 53; birth of induced by stones wrapped in cloth, 59; special names given to, 70; visitor must locate mummies of, 120; inquiry into practices concerning, 168-71

Chinchacocha (Chinchaycocha), province, visited by Dr. Ramírez, 14; mentioned, 70, 139

Chinchas, town, 88

Chiriguanáes Indians, near Potosí, 149

Chochas, town, 82

fasting, by guardians of fields, 36; eating only white corn and meat, 54; priest to be informed of, 173

Ferrer, Father Raphael, 148

festivals, begin with chicha, 41; llamas sacrificed, 42; practices at, 47-48; at beginning of the rainy season, 49; celebrated when a child is named, 53; at time of child's first haircut, 54; at time of putting on breechclout, 55; Acotay mita, 58; during eclipse of moon, 59; Oncoy mita, about time of Corpus Christi, 70; used for pagan and Christian purposes, 72; inquiry concerning, 120-21, 170; of Huatachana, 140

Francisco, Dominican friar also known as Francisco or Miguel Cano, burned and removed huacas, 25; destroyed gifts to huacas, 27; mentioned, 26, 81, 84, 85, 86, 88, 89, 161

Frías Herrán, Juan de, Father Provincial, 6

García Cabello, Father Joseph, Augustinian friar, 162

García Quadrado, Alonso, visitor, 80

Garcilaso de la Vega, el Inca, *Anales* of cited, 59

garments and shawls, used for idolatry, 11; mummies dressed in, 16; ornaments for described, 69;

gods, household, called conopas, described, 28; how preserved and worshiped, 29; used to protect irrigation ditches, 30; mentioned *passim*

Gonçález, Father Friar Domingo, 162

Gorgor, mission of, 51

Hernández Príncipe, Licenciate Rodrigo, 80, 85, 112, 143

Huacaibamba, town, 148

Huacho, town near headland of Huara, 37, 52, 64, 95

Hualla, armless stone giant found in, 84

Huamachuco, province in bishopric of Trujillo, 26

Huamalíes, assigned to Dr. Avila, 17, 140, 147

Huamanga, town, 75, 147, 150, 157

Huancaraime, town, 76

Huánuco, town, assigned to Dr. Avila, 17; fine climate in, 147; mentioned, 148

Huarás, town in valley of Huaylas, 19; etymological connection with breechclout suggested, 55

Huarochirí, province, 10, 13, 18, 70, 75, 140

Huascar, son of Topo Inca, 26; orders destruction of temple of Catequilla, 27

Huatachana, festival and assembly, 140

Huaylas, province, 17, 19, 26, 120

Huaylla Cayan, town, 87, 88

Humi, town, 82

Humayan, place called, 88

Hupa, ancient town, 86

Iulí, town, 160

Jaen, city, Indians paid tribute in espingo there, 44; mentioned, 150

Jíbaro Indians, 151

Lampas, town, 90

languages, Indian, mistranslation of Bible into, 61; priests' ignorance of, 62, 93; mass should be sung in, 102; Quechua and Aymara named as most important, 160

lightning, worship of as Líbiac (or Hillapa), 23; sacrifices to insure harvest, 31, 85; twins so named, 51; inquiry concerning, 166; forbidden as name, 169, 170

Vaca, Governor Diego, entered territory of Maina, Jíbaro, and Cocamama Indians, 150
Valencia, Don Pedro de, bishop of Chuquiavo, 78
Valera, Father Blas, cited by Garcilaso de la Vega, 59
Vázquez, Father Joan, principal of school for caciques, 150
vessels, used for drinking chicha, 19; variety described, 69; buried, 83; inquiry concerning, 122

Virves, Licentiate Francisco de, 83
Visca, town in province of Yauyos, 13

Xampai, town, 51
Xauxa(s) (Xaujas), province, 13, 18, 75

Yámor, town, huaca representing lightning removed from, 85
Yauyos, province, 13, 18

www.ingramcontent.com/pod-product-compliance
Lightning Source LLC
Chambersburg PA
CBHW031508270326
41930CB00006B/301